GS 1220

THE
PASSING WINTER

A sequel to *Seeds of Hope*

CHURCH HOUSE PUBLISHING

Church House Publishing
Church House
Great Smith Street
London SW1P 3NZ

ISBN 0 7151 3797 2

Published 1996 by Church House Publishing

Cover design by Peggy Chapman

Printed in England by the Longdunn Press Ltd, Bristol

Contents

Acknowledgements

The Committee for Minority Ethnic Anglican Concerns is very appreciative of the support which has been given by the House of Bishops and several diocesan bishops towards the development of this work. This was evidenced in the second diocesan progress reports, when CMEAC's *Seeds of Hope* Advisory Group received 100 per cent response from the dioceses.

The Committee is also very grateful to its network: the diocesan Link People and the Young Minority Ethnic Anglican Group for their commitment which has helped to heighten awareness of the issues in many dioceses.

The *Seeds of Hope* Advisory Group members who were involved in preparing this report on behalf of the Committee were:

>   The Revd Theo Samuel (Chairman of Advisory Group)
>
>   The Rt Revd Colin Buchanan
>
>   The Revd Rajinder Daniel
>
>   Mr Charles Severs
>
>   Mrs Glynne Gordon-Carter (drafted the report)
>
>   Miss Gillian Bloor (typed the report)

CMEAC's *Seeds of Hope* Advisory Group has worked assiduously over the last five years in order to monitor the response and progress of the Church at the national and diocesan levels to *Seeds of Hope*. The members of the Advisory Group were:

The Revd Theo Samuel	Mrs Gloria Rich
The Revd Rajinder Daniel	The Rt Revd Dr John Sentamu
The Very Revd Robert Jeffery	Mr Charles Severs
The Revd Eileen Lake	Mr Nigel Barnett (General Synod Office)
Sister Patsy Peart	Mrs Glynne Gordon-Carter (CMEAC's Secretary)

Foreword

In my Presidential address to the General Synod in November 1991, a day after the General Synod's debate and the overwhelming endorsement of the report, *Seeds of Hope*, by the then Committee for Black Anglican Concerns, I called on the Church to set three priorities for the Quinquennium. Namely, **Confidence** in the message we proclaim, **Evangelism** in its Anglican multi-faceted way, and the urgent need to deal with our internal **Unity**.

This sequel to *Seeds of Hope*, *The Passing Winter*, clearly demonstrates the need for the Church to recognise that there are plenty of good things going on to encourage us and give us confidence. The work of the Committee has been undoubtedly one of the ways in which God has been blessing his Church. The genuine emerging visibility of minority ethnic Anglicans since the Committee was formed, nearly ten years ago, is a clear sign of the 'passing winter', but I am aware there is still much to be done; and I long for the day when every member of our Church will have the freedom to exercise the God-given abilities they possess.

The Lord of the Church, whose Gospel is both inclusive and liberating, asks of us to celebrate our unity in diversity and to address most urgently our perceptions of **leadership, worship** and **concepts of power**.

Racism has no part in the Christian Gospel. It contradicts our Lord's command to love our neighbours as ourselves. It offends the fundamental Christian belief that every person is made in the image of God and is equally precious in his sight. It solves no problems and creates nothing but hatred and fear.

Every Christian person in every generation has an individual responsibility to oppose and resist racism in all its forms, striving to reflect that divine love which alone fills our lives with meaning and hope.

The themes of justice and the God-given human worth link the separate chapters of this sequel in a way which gives us hope and challenges our complacency, our prejudices, and our misconceptions.

The twenty-seven recommendations, given under three main headings – to the **Dioceses** and their **Structures**, to the **Parishes** and to the **General Synod Boards and Councils** – suggest further what the Church should be doing at all levels in order to give a positive and stronger response to the task of combating racism; and at the same time affirm, encourage and heighten awareness.

It is my privilege as Archbishop of Canterbury to commend to you this sequel to *Seeds of Hope*, which represents the fruit of five years' commitment and hard work by the Committee for Minority Ethnic Anglican Concerns (formerly known as the Committee for Black Anglican Concerns).

+ George Cantuar

Michaelmas 1996

Preface

The work of the *Seeds of Hope* Advisory Group has been set in the context of rising racism in Britain and in the rest of Europe. It is also set in the context of the high expectation, particularly on the part of the minority ethnic communities, that the Church will address matters of social justice as a part of its mission and ministry.

In Britain, as in the rest of Europe, physical violence and verbal abuse is the daily experience of members of minority ethnic communities. Who can forget the experience of Stephen Lawrence, an 18-year old student, stabbed to death while waiting for a bus in South East London? Or Shiji Lapite, who died in police custody a few months ago. The sad fact is that in Urban Priority Areas the stresses and strains of the struggle for a life with basic human dignity are just as intense as that depicted in the *Faith in the City* report of 1985. This, in its turn, has increased the spiral of violence, and has meant that the minority communities have become more vulnerable than ever. Of course, violence is not the only way in which racism continues to express itself. Minority communities continue to be at the bottom of the economic ladder; unemployment rates are high - in London, for instance, Government figures show that over 60% of 'black' young people are unemployed. The Asylum and Immigration Act (1996) has created a pool of those who will continue to need the help of the community at large.

The picture, however, is not all one of gloom. We thank God for a number of significant advances made over the years – for the containment of the extremist political parties, for the greater understanding expressed by the leadership of metropolitan police forces on race issues (though much more needs to be done at the local level), for the implementation of Equal Opportunity Policies in the major institutions of our country as standard procedure, for the general support on the part of large sections of the British public for the idea that we now live in a multi-ethnic, multi-cultural and multi-faith society. Part of this scene of encouragement is the contribution made by the Church of England in its willingness to relate to issues of racial justice, both internally and externally. The Advisory Committee feels heartened by the willingness of the leadership in the dioceses we have visited to look at their structures and accommodate the changes that we have recommended, to facilitate the greater participation and representation of Anglicans from minority ethnic communities.

The second context of the work of the *Seeds of Hope* Advisory Group is the expectation of Christians from the minority ethnic communities. This expectation stems from an acute awareness that as God has revealed himself to be deeply concerned about matters of social justice, the Church must also order its own affairs in such a way that it seeks, relentlessly, passionately, to express the attributes of that 'just society' internally, so that it can more easily relate to the injustices in the world around us.

This dual context has guided the work of the Advisory Group, whether it be the advising of the dioceses on their responses to racism, or working with other departments of General Synod in producing resources to enable the process of education, which is a necessary prerequisite for the changing of attitudes, to take place, or efforts to enable dioceses to develop, implement and monitor Equal Opportunity Policies. We are grateful for the goodwill and co-operation that we have invariably received from the Boards and Councils of General Synod, and the leadership of the Church of England, both centrally and in the dioceses.

The contexts also enable us to see that, alas, the work of the Committee for Minority Ethnic Anglican Concerns continues to be needed. The winter is not yet over. There are those who still feel the icy blasts of racism beating at their very doors. We will continue to enable the Church of England to work for their protection until the winter is passed, as it surely will. 'Thy Kingdom come, O Lord'.

The Revd Theo Samuel
Chairman of the *Seeds of Hope* Advisory Group

The Message

The Black Anglican Celebration for the Decade of Evangelism at York in July 1994 marked a watershed of change for both the minority ethnic Anglicans and the majority ethnic Anglicans. The 'seeds of hope' sown since 1987 have been patiently but deliberately watered and nourished in the Church of England by a huge majority of people who have taken to heart the words of Micah 6: 8:

> He has told you, O mortal, what is good: and what does the Lord require of you but to do justice, and to love kindness, and to walk humbly with your God.

As a community of faith we are learning very slowly not to take ourselves too seriously by focusing our eyes on the freedom offered in the Gospel in terms of freedom for openness, oneness, newness and truth.

The Trumpet Call at the York Celebration encapsulated what Black Anglicans have always demanded of the Church of England and its leaders, of their English society, of themselves and of God. Namely the determination to remain and participate fully in the task of modelling the Church of England on what heaven is like, which is the most urgent call of all Anglicans. And for many Black Anglicans who were frozen out of their Church, these past nine years have seen the memories of courtship for the Gospel, a courtship started by the English missionaries to Black people, as in the Song of Solomon Chapter two, verses 10-11, slowly returning:

> My beloved speaks and says to me: "Arise, my love, my fair one, and come away; for now the winter is past, and the rain is over and gone. The flowers appear on the earth; the time of singing has come, and the voice of the turtledove is heard in our land."

The promise of Jeremiah 30: 17 is slowly being realised: *'I will restore health to you, and your wounds I will heal'*. But any healing process to be effective requires sustained application of appropriate medication, a healing environment and appropriate sustenance.

There is a lot of good that has happened and for this we give thanks. But we must ensure that the seeds which were sown in winter clearly face the spring and the promise of a warm summer. And my message to all readers of this report is simply this:

First, in the words of John Curran, in a speech on the Right of Election of Lord Mayor of Dublin, 10 July 1790, *'The condition upon which God hath given liberty to man is eternal vigilance, which condition if he break, servitude is at once the consequence of his crime, and the punishment of his guilt'*. Let us, therefore *'Be sober, be vigilant, because our adversary the devil, as a roaring lion, walketh about, seeking whom he may devour'* (1 Peter 5: 8). And the demon of racism (the theory, prejudice and practice which advantages or disadvantages people solely on the grounds of their colour, culture or ethnic origin) has devoured many and enslaved its minions.

Secondly, the instruments for combating racism in Church and Nation must help all the foot-soldiers to maintain **mobility** and **flexibility**. *'New wine for new wine-skins'*. Our language must be contemporary. That is why the Committee for Black Anglican Concerns has been deliberately re-named The Committee for Minority Ethnic Anglican Concerns. The word 'Black' in twentieth century multi-ethnic Britain is no longer inclusive or useful for all minority ethnic people in the country who face racism in all its varied forms. The parallel term here is the word **man.** Let the reader understand.

Thirdly, the Church must be at the **cutting-edge of a healing mission**. In the words of the Magnificat this means the Church must be (1) **PRO-JUSTICE:** *'he has put down the mighty from their thrones, and has exalted the humble and meek'*; (2) **PRO-PEOPLE:** *'He has regarded the lowliness of his handmaid'*; (3) **PRO-LIFE:** not in the narrow sense of protecting the life of the unborn child – but life in all its fullness: *'He has filled the hungry with good things and has sent the rich empty away'*.

Finally, a church that is experiencing 'the passing winter' needs to embrace and forever hold fast to the Good News, especially as it is expressed in Luke/Acts. For the gospel according to Luke/Acts is (a) the good news of God's justice; (b) the good news of spiritual power; (c) the power to embrace suffering; (d) the power to freely love; (e) the power to redeem humanity; and all of this is made possible by the Holy Spirit who energises, transforms and creates the Church.

What *The Passing Winter* asks of us all is, as we say in Swahili, let us pull together in love: **HARAMBE!**

The Rt Revd Dr John Sentamu
Chairman – CMEAC
Michaelmas 1996

CHAPTER I

Background to this sequel

1.1   In November 1991, *Seeds of Hope: Report of a Survey on Combating Racism in the Dioceses of the Church of England* was launched at a very well attended press conference, and debated by the General Synod (GS). This two-hour debate was very significant because for the first time the General Synod discussed the institutional racism which existed within the structures. The fact that work had to be done by the whole Church through raising awareness in the General Synod, dioceses and parishes was acknowledged. The debate was encouraging as many Synod members spoke firmly of the importance of tackling racism and the need for a change of heart, and practice in the Church. It was acknowledged that this work was just as important in mainly rural dioceses, where there were comparatively few minority ethnic people, as it was in mainly urban dioceses.

1.2   Here are some representative excerpts from the General Synod debate, November Group of Sessions 1991, report of proceedings.

> To challenge our racism we have to take this report seriously in every diocese. It is as important in the white dioceses where there are comparatively few black and Asian people as it is in the urban dioceses. (p. 817: Archdeacon Stephen Lowe of Sheffield)

> The situation will not improve until we as a Church are willing to talk, to discuss, to deal with those areas where there is hidden racism. (p. 812: Dr Sentamu)

> It is also a matter of white Anglican concerns, it is a white problem and must be addressed by white people. I wish to sound a note of caution about what has happened elsewhere, in that very often one will get black people 'rounded up' as it were to do this work. That would be a supreme way of marginalising it. It has to be done by the whole Church. (p. 818: Mr Peter Robinson, Chelmsford)

1.3   Dr John Sentamu, Chairman of the Committee, in asking for the Synod to receive the report spoke of the need in the Church for a change of heart and practice. He said that it would be important to exercise the three gifts given at Pentecost.

> First then let us recognise the gift of repentance and forgiveness; the second needful gift at Pentecost is to speak our mind, express our feelings, tell our experiences in truth and love. Third, the gift of hearing, to become the listener instead of always doing the speaking and deciding what is good for the black person. (pp. 796-7)

1.4   By the end of the debate, the *Seeds of Hope* report was received, and the motions as stated were carried:

> i) That this report be received;

> ii) That this Synod, affirming that all men and women of every hue and ethnic group belong to the one human race, are all made in the image of God and that each is of unique worth in His sight, commends the recommendations in Chapter 5 of the Report for discussion and action as appropriate by Boards and Councils of the General Synod, by dioceses, deaneries and parishes.

1.5   In keeping with its terms of reference, the Committee assumed a monitoring role, as it was felt that the successful debate of the report by General Synod and its commendation to dioceses, deaneries and parishes did not necessarily mean that there would be a prompt response in following up the report.

1.6   In January 1992, Dr Sentamu, the Committee's Chairman, presented a paper to the House of Bishops with respect to their own role in dioceses. He remarked that the General Synod debate on *Seeds of Hope* had indicated a willingness to address seriously race issues throughout the Church, and suggestions were being offered because the Committee was very aware of its responsibility to help dioceses devise ways and means of acting on the recommendations. The Chairman also stated that the Committee would request diocesan progress reports from bishops in 1993 and 1994 as these would enable the Committee to monitor the response to *Seeds of Hope* by dioceses, deaneries and parishes.

1.7   The Chairman also informed bishops that the *Seeds of Hope* Advisory Group had been set up by the Committee in order to offer assistance and support to dioceses. The Revd Theo Samuel was Chairman of the Advisory Group. Dr Sentamu also wrote to General Synod Boards and Councils about their response to *Seeds of Hope.*

Visits to Dioceses

1.8   During the conduct of the survey which led to the *Seeds of Hope* report (1988-91) visits were made by the Survey Team to the following dioceses:

Birmingham	Exeter
Bradford	Lichfield
Chelmsford	London
Chester	Newcastle
Chichester	Southwark
Durham	Southwell

Since the publication and debate of *Seeds of Hope* (1991), teams from the Advisory Group have visited other dioceses, namely:

Hereford	Leicester
Gloucester	Liverpool
Guildford	Manchester

Assignments have also been carried out by various members of the Group at the request of the following dioceses:

Canterbury	Peterborough
Chelmsford	St Albans
Lichfield	Southwark
Liverpool	Winchester
Oxford	York

1.9   In 1997, the Advisory Group will be visiting the Diocese of Carlisle. CMEAC is actively pursuing possibilities for other diocesan visits in 1997-98.

Why a Sequel?

1.10   Five years on from *Seeds of Hope* we now report to the Synod believing that there has been an emerging visibility of minority ethnic Anglicans since this Committee was formed.

We are attempting to fulfil the following tasks:

(a)   to record the progress made by the Church of England in the task of combating racism since the General Synod debate on the report in November 1991;

(b)   to provide an overview and understanding of how the work is being tackled by dioceses;

(c)   to provide examples of good practice which will be of value to other dioceses, deaneries and parishes;

(d)   to support those dioceses which are finding the task of addressing the issues hard going, also to encourage them to learn from dioceses of a similar profile which are tackling the issues effectively;

(e)   to identify further what the Church should be doing in order to give a positive and stronger response to the task of combating racism in its structures.

1.11   In preparing *The Passing Winter* the Advisory Group considered factors such as action which had been taken by the diocese since the publication of *Seeds of Hope*; the extent to which there were proper strategies in existence for tackling racism; action which was planned; the level of participation by minority ethnic Anglicans in the structures; the relationship of the diocesan Committee/Group to the structures; the existence of diocesan equal opportunities policies and their implementation; also the links which exist between the dioceses and CMEAC.

Good Practice

1.12   The need for good practice was highlighted by Mrs Appelbee in her contribution to the General Synod debate on the report when she said:

Seeds of Hope points usefully to some good practice, but more good practice needs to be developed, and this can only be done when we go away prepared to struggle with the issue in our own patch and develop the appropriate good practice. (p. 800: Mrs Elaine Appelbee, Bradford)

1.13   *The Passing Winter* will show that in some dioceses there is good practice in certain aspects, and these will be mentioned as appropriate. However, the report will also show that a great deal more needs to be done at diocesan, deanery and parish levels in order to ensure that there is real growth of the *Seeds of Hope*, and a harvest in the Church of England.

CHAPTER II

Recommendations to dioceses from *Seeds of Hope*

2.1.   We believe that the Church's mission must include combating racism among its members and within its structures at every level. A British society that is already multi-ethnic and multi-cultural, in which there are now other faith communities present, is the arena in which the Church must live its loyalty to Jesus Christ. The issues which are being raised are central to the Church's understanding and important for its witness in contemporary life. (*Seeds of Hope*, 5.1)

2.2   We believe that there are in fact seven areas of work which need to be clearly identified as separate issues. These are as follows:-

(A)   The diocese and its commitment to combating racism through its structures (paras. 5.3-5.21).

(B)   The role of the Diocesan Board of Education in combating racism (paras. 5.22-5.28).

(C)   The participation of black people within the life of the Church (paras. 5.29-5.36).

(D)   The Church as an employer - its commitment to equal opportunity (paras. 5.37-5.42).

(E)   Relationships with other black Christians (paras. 5.43-5.44).

(F)   Relationships with people of other faiths (paras. 5.45-5.46).

(G)   Racial justice issues within the wider society (paras. 5.47-5.49).

The priority to be given to each will vary from diocese to diocese: the vital thing is that they should not be confused, or neglected. (*Seeds of Hope*, 5.2)

First Diocesan Progress Reports

2.3   In 1993, the Committee received progress reports from 26 dioceses, in response to the Chairman's request to the House of Bishops. Several dioceses had taken the recommendations seriously; in fact, in some instances CMEAC was sent very useful information on strategies which were being implemented. The response was varied, as dioceses sought to develop work based on their particular situation. It must be borne in mind that, when *Seeds of Hope* was debated in 1991, some dioceses were beyond the starting line, others were at the starting line, and some had not yet got to the starting line. The information provided in the progress reports in 1993 reflected that situation, as some dioceses still did not consider this work a matter of priority or urgency.

2.4   The Dioceses of Derby and Newcastle had analysed the situation in their dioceses by using the headings from *Seeds of Hope*, Chapter V. Other dioceses had initiated action by having a debate on *Seeds of Hope* at their diocesan synod, namely Birmingham, Bristol, Chester, Manchester, Oxford, Southwark, Ripon, St Albans, Sheffield and York.

2.5   Following on from the diocesan debates, in some dioceses (e.g. Oxford) the Bishop's Council had proceeded to set up a working party with specific terms of reference. Some dioceses (e.g. Liverpool) had immediately commended the report to parishes and deaneries for action: some had formulated an equal opportunity policy; others had built up a support group around the CBAC diocesan Link Persons which reported to Bishop's Council (e.g. Chester and Guildford). Following on from *Seeds of Hope* debates, some dioceses were holding racism awareness training beginning with the Bishop's Council (e.g. Birmingham). This training was held on the principle that the leaders of the dioceses should set a precedent. The Diocese of Liverpool supplied copies of *Seeds of Hope* to all clergy.

2.6   The first progress reports displayed a variety of initiatives dependent on their profile and the extent to which these matters had been addressed in the past. In general, dioceses with a larger percentage of minority ethnic Anglicans were in the forefront and pursued more active strategies.

2.7   We recognise that changes in diocesan bishops and diocesan structures may hamper progress, but it is nevertheless disappointing to report that in one or two cases dioceses with a strong minority ethnic component have been notably tardy.

Second Diocesan Progress Reports

2.8   The request for the second progress report which was delayed until 1995 achieved 100 per cent response from the dioceses. These second diocesan progress reports showed considerable improvement over the 1993 reports, as more dioceses were taking this work seriously.

2.9   This could be due to many reasons: the support of bishops, as well as key people in some dioceses; the relationship which CMEAC had developed with the House of Bishops whereby the Committee consulted the bishops on major pieces of work in advance in order to get their views and support; the commitment of the CMEAC diocesan network; and not least the impact of the 1994 Black Anglican Celebration for the Decade of Evangelism.

An integrated approach is essential

2.10   Every diocese should strive to achieve an integrated approach which allows the work of the Diocesan Minority Ethnic Committee to act as a critique for the work of the Boards and Councils.

2.11   We would recommend that dioceses make a conscious effort to work at integrated action in response to *Seeds of Hope* concerns, across and through diocesan structures. The Bishop of Liverpool's contribution to the 1991 General Synod debate on *Seeds of Hope* made reference to the role of diocesan structures.

We need a repentance, a leaving behind of patterns which are no longer right. That means making space for black people, as we said in Faith in the City, *in Synod, in dioceses and deanery synods, our Boards and Committees here and in the dioceses. I believe that this report can usefully be looked at by every board and committee in our diocese ... by the Board of Education for Governors in schools, by directors of continuing ministerial education for clergy, by directors of adult education.* (p. 805: Bishop of Liverpool, The Rt Revd David Sheppard)

2.12   Dioceses such as Birmingham, Coventry, Leicester, Liverpool, Oxford and Ripon have identified the role of their diocesan bodies in carrying out this work. The Support Group in Chester has drawn up a Mission Statement for the diocese. Every diocese should strive for an integrated approach. The role of the Committee is to stimulate and encourage this work – *not* to do it.

CHAPTER III

The dioceses and their commitment to combating racism through the structures

Diocesan Structures

3.1   As far as diocesan structures were concerned, 24 dioceses had set up committees or groups responsible for combating racism by 1996. The majority of these committees report to the Bishop's Council or the Council/Board for Social Responsibility. In fact these included dioceses which, prior to *Seeds of Hope*, had no structures in place and had little if any intention to address these issues. There are various models in the dioceses: e.g. in York the Diocesan Committee for Black Anglican Concerns is chaired by the Bishop of Selby; in the case of Manchester, the Chairman of the Minority Ethnic Group is serving on the Bishop's Council as an ex-officio member; in Birmingham, the Bishop's Adviser is a member of staff of the Board of Ministries; in Leicester Diocese, the Bishop's Adviser on Race attends the bishop's staff meeting. In Oxford, the chair of the Diocesan Race Group is a member of the Bishop's Council.

3.2   The Dioceses of Leicester and Liverpool have made deliberate attempts to recruit minority ethnic Anglicans to serve as members of Boards, Councils and Committees. In Leicester, minority ethnic Anglicans are serving on the following Boards: Finance, Education, Mission and Social Responsibility, and the Advisory Board of Ministry. This has been achieved either by constitutional changes, co-option or effective sponsorship of candidates for election. In Liverpool, minority ethnic people have been identified to serve on the Boards of Education, Ministry, Mission and Unity, Pastoral Committee, Social Responsibility and Urban Priority Areas.

Resources

STAFFING

3.3.   The Dioceses of Birmingham, Chelmsford, Coventry, Derby, Gloucester, Leicester, Lichfield, Manchester, Oxford, Ripon, Sheffield, Southwark and Winchester have appointed persons in various capacities to help to focus thinking and action in the diocese. However, most are appointed on a part-time basis. Again, we would urge that where there is an officer, that person should be on a par with other Heads of Departments/Boards. This will help to prevent marginalisation of the work. The Social Responsibility Officer or Board for Social Responsibility is in charge of this work in six dioceses

3.4   Job titles vary from diocese to diocese: Diocesan Race Relations Adviser, Community Relations Officer, Adviser for Black Ministry, Bishop's Adviser on Black Concerns are some of the titles used. Twenty-nine dioceses have set out their plans for future work; in some dioceses, especially where there is an officer specifically employed for this role, the programme of work is more focused.

FUNDING

3.5   In a few dioceses adequate funding has been provided for this work, but in some there is still a lack of proper secretarial support, and this hampers progress. Southwark Diocese, which has a Commission, has assigned full-time officers to each episcopal area within the diocese; Oxford Diocese has appointed race relations officers in two archdeaconries; and Derby has two part-time posts. We are aware of financial constraints in the dioceses, though where there is real commitment we are confident that the resources will be provided.

TRAINING WITHIN THE STRUCTURES

3.6   With respect to racism awareness training, Archdeacon Stephen Lowe made the following suggestions in the General Synod debate: '...that all diocesan senior staff meetings submit themselves to racism awareness training. This should include diocesan secretaries. Unless those responsible for managing the structures become aware of their racism, they cannot combat it'. (p. 817: The Archdeacon of Sheffield)

3.7   There are several examples of good practice in the dioceses with respect to training within the structures. We would like to acknowledge some of the work which has been done, or which is being planned.

Birmingham	The Bishop's Council undertook racism awareness training.
Blackburn	A racism awareness module was offered for clergy in post-ordination training.
Bradford	The diocese is exploring the possibility for a more substantial input on race issues within their Diocesan Lay Foundation Course.
Canterbury	The diocese is considering racism awareness training.
Chelmsford	The prospectus of the North Thames Ministerial Training Course includes a module on culture.
Coventry	Equal opportunity policy (EOP) training days have been held for EOP Group/Training, Heads of Departments and Bishop's Staff. They are planning EOP training for rural deans/lay chairs. They are also preparing materials for racism awareness training.
Exeter	An inter-denominational team of eight people has had anti-racist training and has made available a package of presentations on race relations to ministry training courses, local Christian Churches and others. A resource bank (booklets, videos, Bible studies etc.) has been built up.
Leicester	Bishop's staff has had training in racism awareness, training will be offered to Bishop's Council as well as rural deans.
Lichfield	Racism awareness training is being planned.

Liverpool	A race awareness day has been held for senior officers.
Manchester	The Minority Ethnic Group has been trained in racism awareness.
Ripon	EOP training has been provided for bishop's staff, rural deans, deanery lay chairpersons and Chairperson and Executive officers of main diocesan Boards. The Race and Interfaith Committee of the Board for Mission and Unity is planning training days.
Sheffield	Diocesan staff undertook racism awareness training.
Rochester	A race awareness training day is being planned.
St Albans	Members of the Community and Race Group have undertaken Methodist Leadership Racism Awareness Workshops (MELRAW) training.

3.8   Several dioceses reported on the great difficulty which they experience in getting people to attend racism awareness and equal opportunity policy seminars. One bishop stated: *'We are experiencing enormous difficulty in persuading people to come to them, but of the two pilot workshops which we have now held, both have gone well and have been well received once people got there.'*

3.9   In a few dioceses, the Bishop's Council or the Bishop's staff has taken a lead in undertaking training in racism awareness. We hope that this strategy will be emulated by all dioceses. The diocese also has a responsibility to ensure that training in these matters is provided in post-ordination, in-service and lay training programmes.

Theological Colleges, Courses, Readers and Local Training Schemes

3.10   With respect to these colleges, the Committee is of the opinion that colleges need to make more conscious efforts to include in the curricula for ordinands training in preparation for ministry in a multi-ethnic, multi-faith and multi-cultural society. We are aware of the initiatives which have been carried out by some colleges. The Advisory

Board of Ministry (ABM) has shown its commitment to this work through some of its publications/papers. Special reference must be made of the ABM paper on 'Race' in *Theological Education: An Audit for Use by Colleges and Courses* as it offers theological colleges an holistic approach to the task of combating racism. In practice, we strongly recommend that theological colleges and courses include a module within their curricula on race and racial justice issues. These institutions should seek ways of collaborating with the Simon of Cyrene Theological Institute. All ministers of the Gospel must be trained for the ministry of the Church in its multi-faceted Anglican Communion way – recognising and valuing cultural and ethnic diversity.

3.11   Training in 'race' and racial justice issues is of the utmost importance because clergy sometimes find themselves in difficult situations which they are not able to handle, as their training did not equip them fully. In that connection, the dioceses need to utilise training which is available through the Simon of Cyrene Theological Institute. This is an initiative which has been set up and is being funded by the Church of England, for its use as well as the use of other denominations. *'The Institute is a centre not just for cross-cultural encounter between black and white christians but aims to be a place for the stimulation of theological thinking and action from the perspective, culture and experience(s) of black people'* (Institute's Prospectus).

Vocations

3.12   With respect to black clergy, some comments which were expressed in *Seeds of Hope* bear repetition in *The Passing Winter*. There still seems to be a perception around that minority ethnic clergy should or would only work in parishes with substantial minority ethnic people. Dioceses in fact should be consciously attracting minority ethnic clergy. Like their white colleagues, these clergy value a width of ministerial experience. This will include some parishes with substantial minority ethnic communities and some without. They should be encouraged and invited to work in parishes of all types.

3.13   Patrons, including bishops, should make a point of considering minority ethnic clergy for senior positions in the dioceses. Young people obviously need to see role models if vocations to the ministry are to be nurtured, and congregations need to be familiar with minority ethnic people exercising leadership skills within the Church, otherwise the Church will be regarded as having a hidden racist agenda. We note that steps have been taken to remedy this situation since the publication of *Seeds of Hope*, and the Church of England now has three minority ethnic bishops. We are encouraged by the successful efforts which were made by ABM and diocesan bishops towards increasing the number of minority ethnic selectors. Some dioceses, e.g. Birmingham, Chelmsford, Leicester and Oxford, have recruited vocations advisers from among minority ethnic Anglicans in order to encourage vocations, lay and ordained.

3.14   The Dioceses of Birmingham and Chelmsford stand out with respect to the work which is being done to encourage vocations. In the case of Birmingham, the Adviser for Black Ministries has the responsibility to ensure the development for lay education and training. The Adviser was involved in a training day called by the Bishop of Birmingham in October 1995 for clergy in parishes with minority ethnic Anglicans. Three lay members of the Board of Ministries are minority ethnic Anglicans and there has been a small increase in the number of minority ethnic Readers and clergy.

3.15   With respect to Chelmsford, the Officer for the Standing Conference on Race has as part of his responsibility the encouragement of vocations, lay and ordained. Currently twelve minority ethnic people are in training from that diocese, in the following areas:

> Ordination 3
> Readers 3
> Christian Studies leading to Bishop's Certificate 6

Diocesan and Deanery Synods.

3.16   We understand that by 1996, 16 dioceses had debated *Seeds of Hope* and the report was being followed up in various ways. Appendix

A provides examples of diocesan resolutions. At the request of some dioceses, members of the *Seeds of Hope* Advisory Group assisted with the formulation of some diocesan synod motions. The Chairman, members of the Committee, as well as the Secretary were invited to speak at various diocesan synod debates. Several dioceses had not debated the report; instead, in some, there were discussions by Bishop's Council, as this was regarded by the dioceses concerned as the best way to progress the report.

3.17   Overall, very few deanery synods have debated the report. However, in some deaneries, e.g. in the Dioceses of Chelmsford, Chester and Oxford, *Seeds of Hope* has been on the agenda. In Oxford, feedback on *Seeds of Hope* was the main agenda item at one deanery synod and each parish was allocated two minutes for summary reports of their PCC's discussion and plans. The Brent Deanery Chapter in London Diocese invited CMEAC's Secretary to address one of their meetings. Various members of the Committee, diocesan Link Persons and other people have spoken at many parish, deanery and diocesan meetings.

The Diocesan Board of Education

3.18   Currently in some dioceses there appears to be more of an awareness of the need to educate the school community on these issues in whatever area they are located; however, goodwill must be translated into action in order to counter racial harassment and violence in schools. Anti-racist policies and equal opportunity policies which are formulated should be owned by the head teacher, governors, teaching, ancillary, administrative and support staff, as well as pupils and parents. So although we would be the first to acknowledge that there is good practice in some schools, which we hope is being shared with other schools, there is still a great deal of work to be done in all our Church schools, primary as well as secondary.

3.19   In some dioceses it is commendable that some schools have taken great care to formulate fair admission, anti-racist and equal opportunities policies. However, they will only be effective if implemented. There are still harrowing stories alleging the non-admission of minority ethnic children to some Church schools. The Committee is also very concerned about the number of minority ethnic children who are being excluded from schools and would ask Church schools to monitor their own situation. The alleged disproportionate over-representation of black pupils among those excluded from schools was a priority for the Commission for Racial Equality (CRE) in 1995. The Commission developed a research programme to identify the principal elements of good practice in schools where there has been a reduction in exclusion rates. In November 1996, the CRE will publish a report on exclusion of black pupils. By March 1997, the Commission will publish a Code of Good Practice.

3.20   Recent research by Child Line which led to the report *Children and Racism* has identified an increase in racist bullying.

> *The most common problem among the 1,616 children who called and identified themselves as black was that their lives were being blighted by racism both inside and outside the classroom. The Director of Child Line also said that the relentless persecution meant that their self esteem was battered. Child Line stated that [all] schools [including Church schools] need to ensure that anti-racism is part of their policy to stop bullying generally and that work needs to be carried through to the curriculum to raise awareness and promote the prevention of racist bullying.*

3.21   Schools need to make a concerted effort to recruit teachers from minority ethnic communities, as well as to explore the possibilities of appointing foundation governors from these communities. In some dioceses, Boards of Education are very aware of the issues and are concerned enough to set up strategies to address them. We acknowledge the fact that some issues would be more relevant in some dioceses than others; however, this should not be used as an excuse to do nothing. Part of the agenda of school governors should be the monitoring and reporting on these issues on a regular basis.

3.22   Examples are provided of some of the initiatives which have been taken in some dioceses with respect to education issues which impact on minority ethnic communities. In Liverpool, the Diocesan

Committee for Black Anglican Concerns has held discussions with the Board of Education on the following issues: exclusion of black pupils; the difficulty of recruiting black people as school governors; admission policies. The Race and Community Officer in Leicester Diocese has been in dialogue with the Diocesan Director of Education (DDE) on the subject of Church schools and the composition of governing bodies, particularly in relation to foundation governors.

3.23   One of Derby's aided schools has played a leading role in the development of a racial harassment policy. The staff of the Southwark Race Relations Commission is involved in working with schools. The Board of Education in Exeter is promoting multi-cultural work in schools. Gloucester's Community and Race Relations Committee researched and produced a report on race and prejudice in Gloucester schools. This became the lead paper for the Commission for Racial Equality's report entitled *Learning in Terror.* Carlisle's Diocesan Board of Education has produced a paper on race and culture which has been circulated to schools.

3.24   As part of its commitment to raising awareness on racism, the General Synod Board of Education's National Society has published a booklet entitled *Respect for All: Developing Anti-racist Policies in a Church School.* This booklet was the result of two seminars entitled 'Racial Violence in School and Society: The Role of the Church School', which were held in 1992. These seminars were jointly sponsored by the National Society, CMEAC, the Roman Catholic Church, the Methodist Church, the Council of Churches for Britain and Ireland (CCBI) Churches' Commission for Racial Justice (CCRJ), and the Commission for Racial Equality (CRE).

3.25   In response to *Seeds of Hope,* the Southwark Diocesan Board of Education 'established a working party to investigate those areas in school life where racism may be present and to offer to schools, their governors and staff strategies for combating racism'. This resulted in the publication *Colour and Spice: Guidance on Combating Racism in Church Schools.*

3.26   Each publication makes a distinctive contribution in the sound and practical support which it offers towards combating racism within the context of the Church school.

3.27   Currently, CMEAC is working collaboratively with the National Society on the development of a project on anti-racist/equal opportunity resources for mainly rural Church schools. This has arisen from the realisation that there are resources available for urban and inner city schools through some diocesan Boards of Education, the LEAs, and agencies such as the Runnymede Trust. However, there is a paucity of relevant material for mainly rural primary schools. This project is being done in collaboration with the DDEs from the ten most rural dioceses and the National Rural Officer. Demand for these resources has been expressed mainly by the Dioceses of Carlisle, Exeter, Hereford and Truro.

3.28   Teacher training in higher education or in schools should continue to develop courses in anti-racism and equal opportunities as an integral part of their curricula, as much greater awareness is needed in professional training and development. This would assist teachers in responding more positively to cultural diversity. Given the significant role which teachers play in educating and training young citizens, we would hope that by way of reinforcement these issues are included in their in-service training at primary and secondary levels.

Diocesan Communication Departments

3.29   We are aware of assistance which has been offered by several diocesan communication officers/departments in different ways towards the development of this work. The General Synod Communications Unit in particular helped with the 1994 Black Anglican Celebration for the Decade of Evangelism. Before and after the Celebration, communication officers were in contact with CMEAC Link Persons and others with respect to local radio and TV interviews. From time to time articles written by bishops and also Link Persons have appeared in several diocesan newsletters/magazines; for this we are grateful, as the role of the communication officers is vital in the task of educating people on race and racial justice issues in the diocese, deanery and parish.

3.30 We would hope that this situation will be remedied, and also wish to reiterate that in order to be focused and systematic 'various means of communicating with parishes should be considered by the appropriate committee with a view towards determining the most effective method within the diocese' (*Seeds of Hope*, 5.20). Where the need arises, minority ethnic people are very willing to be consulted on race-related matters. CMEAC has a network of diocesan Link Persons in 42 dioceses.

Diocesan Resource Centre

3.31 The role of the diocesan resource centre should not be underestimated as this is 'yet another channel through which people at all levels can be educated on multi-ethnic, multi-cultural and inter-faith matters' (*Seeds of Hope*, 5.20). We hope that these centres will make conscious efforts to build up a stock of resources, e.g. videos, study packs, publications, which would be suitable for children and young people, as well as adults. CMEAC hopes that those centres will seek to update their resources from the Bibliography and Resources sections at the end of this report, and from Appendix B in *Seeds of Hope*.

3.32 With respect to visual aids, all diocesan Boards, Councils, Committees and resource centres should ensure that publications, reports, posters, videos, slide presentations and other visual aids reflect the diversity which exists in the Church of England. Materials must project a multi-cultural identity and avoid negative stereotypical images of minority ethnic people. In certain quarters there is some awareness, but this needs to be more evident in the materials which are published at all levels of the dioceses, and indeed the entire Church.

The Church as Employer – its commitment to Equal Opportunity

3.33 During the General Synod debate, Archdeacon Stephen Lowe spoke of the lack of an equal opportunity policy (EOP) for the staff of General Synod. He commented:

I am on the staff committee of this General Synod. It is to our shame that an Equal Opportunities Policy does not yet exist for the Synod. ... We must speed the process up, make it effective and then help dioceses to make sure that they know how to implement an equal opportunities programme within all their employment practice and structures. (p. 817: Archdeacon of Sheffield)

3.34   By 1993, the General Synod Central Board of Finance (CBF) had formulated an equal opportunity policy, as well as a code of practice. Due to its comprehensiveness the policy has served as a model to many dioceses. CBF has set up 'in house' an Equal Opportunity Policy Monitoring Group which has the responsibility for ensuring that the policy is implemented and monitored. The Group is chaired by the personnel officer. Regular reports are given to the General Synod Staff Committee of the Central Board of Finance, the Secretary General, and the General Synod's Staff Association. Training in EOP is being provided for Chairpersons of interviewing panels, as well as staff.

3.35   This awareness of the importance of equal opportunity has also resulted in guidelines being laid down by the General Synod Appointments Sub-Committee in order to help Boards and Councils in appointing members to Working Parties and Committees etc. They are also meant to help guide the Sub-Committee itself in making appointments to subordinate bodies of the Synod.

3.36   CMEAC monitors the dioceses and their commitment to equal opportunity policy on a regular basis. In January 1995, the Committee's *Seeds of Hope* Advisory Group circulated an EOP questionnaire to diocesan secretaries. All dioceses replied. In some dioceses there appeared to be a lack of understanding about the need for a policy. This was borne out by comments such as *'the Bishop and staff responsible for appointments would not discriminate';* or *'there is no immediate intention of formulating or debating such a policy'.* Some dioceses saw equal opportunity only as a race issue, in fact one response stated: *'There are very few ethnic minority people who live in the diocese and there has never been an application from a member of an ethnic minority group for any jobs we have had on offer.'*

3.37   We think that it is important that the policy should be a comprehensive one taking into consideration all aspects: gender, 'race', colour, ethnicity, nationality – including citizenship, disability, age, sexual identity and marital status.

3.38   The following dioceses worked at developing quite comprehensive policies and displayed strengths in various aspects of the policies which they had formulated: Birmingham, Bristol, Chelmsford, Coventry, Liverpool, Ripon and Southwark. The Diocese of Chelmsford took the trouble to examine the theological rationale behind the setting up of an EOP. In 1991, only three dioceses had equal opportunity policies; by 1996, 17 dioceses had policies; some included a code of practice (e.g. Birmingham, Bristol, Coventry and Southwark), and also an EOP Monitoring Group (Coventry, Liverpool and Southwark). Currently three dioceses are working on policies.

3.39   CMEAC's *Seeds of Hope* Advisory Group was not confident that enough was being done to convert the policies into action with respect to implementation, training, monitoring and evaluation, even by dioceses which had good written policies. There was certainly the need for proper procedures to be put in place for monitoring equal opportunity policies, in the majority of dioceses with policies. In most other dioceses which had policies, even there the policies were often inadequate.

3.40   With respect to EOPs, dioceses could be divided into three categories:

(i)   dioceses with policies;

(ii)   dioceses which were working on policies;

(iii)   dioceses without policies, most of whom apparently judged there was no need.

3.41   The Advisory Group recognised that because of the way in which clergy were appointed, it would not be easy to formulate policies; but this was not an impossible situation. The Committee has sought to keep diocesan secretaries informed of developments in EOP, and has responded to dioceses which have requested assistance in formulating and implementing policies. We hope to be given the opportunity to provide an input on equal opportunity at the next annual residential meeting of diocesan secretaries.

3.42   The Advisory Group's main concern has been to encourage fair employment practices, to be supportive of work which is being done to inform on good practice and to encourage dioceses without an EOP to work towards formulating a policy. The Church has a responsibility not only to be fair but to be seen to be fair in its recruitment, employment and training policies.

3.43   The Committee is surprised at why dioceses without equal opportunities policies have not sought to adopt/adapt the policy of the CBF, which in our view is a very good policy, coupled with a monitoring group. Does the independence of each diocese mean that the wheel must be reinvented each time?

3.44   The Committee would also wish to draw attention to the Wood-Sheppard Principles which dealt specifically with race equality in employment. These principles, in the names of Bishop David Sheppard and Bishop Wilfred Wood, have been drawn up and published by the Churches' Commission for Racial Justice and the Race Equality in Employment Project of the Ecumenical Committee for Corporate Responsibility (ECCR).

CHAPTER IV

Responses from parishes
to *Seeds of Hope*

4.1   In reviewing the diocesan progress reports, it is clear that in most areas seeds are being planted; but in order to reap a rich harvest much more work is needed, especially at the parish level, whether there is a large minority ethnic presence or not.

4.2   It must be acknowledged that in some parishes there is good practice; it must also be noted that in most instances these are in inner-city areas. A few mainly rural dioceses are exploring how minority ethnic Anglican concerns *'can be addressed more adequately in a diocese where many parishes mistakenly take the view that this has nothing to do with them'*.

4.3   The Diocesan Officer for Black Anglican Concerns in the Lichfield Diocese circulated a questionnaire on black Anglican concerns through the archdeacon's visitation, and this has been attached as Appendix B. The questionnaire elicited a number of invitations for the adviser to speak to a variety of groups at both parish and deanery levels. The Bishop of Truro asked approximately a dozen parishes in his diocese to obtain copies of the report and to form small study groups in order to discuss the implications and general thinking of *Seeds of Hope.* The Bishop, in his invitation, set eight questions as a suggested framework for study, and these are attached as Appendix C.

4.4   In order to assist parishes, CMEAC has developed a study pack entitled *Seeds of Hope in the Parish* which offers practical guidelines for discussion and action. In some instances, parishes with few or no minority ethnic people have said that 'it is difficult to address the issues of racism in an area where there is such limited experience of black people'. The pack has been prepared bearing their needs in mind as well.

Support for White Clergy

4.5   The role of the clergy continues to be of immense significance in this work. *Seeds of Hope* had posed the question *'How do we get white clergy to bring race issues higher on their agenda?'* Since the publication of that report many clergy have attempted to address these concerns. There are also of course many who have not responded, as they do not consider these issues important to their parochial ministry. Yet *'clergy have great influence on how people perceive themselves and each other in the life of the Church'*. (Comment from Coventry diocesan report)

4.6   The Committee would wish to emphasise that, whether in a mainly inner-city or a rural parish *'clergy need to be properly informed on the nature of our plural society and the implication for ministry within this setting'*. It should also be borne in mind that *'Parochial clergy have a special responsibility to widen people's experiences through preaching and raising issues of racism and racial justice issues'*. (*Seeds of Hope*, 5.11)

Training

4.7   The parish, with the assistance of the diocese, has a special role to play in ensuring that clergy, as well as people exercising other ministries, are trained in racism awareness and racial justice issues. This should be included in post-ordination, in-service and lay training. Some parishes have made a start and have been utilising resources which are available locally as well as nationally.

Support for Black Clergy

4.8   The survey report *How We Stand: a Report on Black Anglican Membership of the Church of England in the 1990s* states that there are 92 minority ethnic clergy in ministry; they are a small number and are a valuable resource for the Church. Like other clergy they must be supported sensitively and pastorally, but it would appear that even more is expected of them than of other clergy, and in fact these clergy face common difficulties in their ministries that few majority ethnic clergy have to deal with. Those who work from minority ethnic communities in parishes with few minority ethnic Anglicans should be offered special support. Readers should also be similarly supported.

Vocations

4.9   The Church still has the uphill task of working at encouraging vocations to ordained ministry among minority ethnic Anglicans, and this should be taken seriously, especially because we are in the Decade of Evangelism. People need to be encouraged to consider selection and training to be lay ministers, Readers and Church Army officers. **Reports received by the Committee from time to time indicate that in some instances clergy discourage rather than encourage minority ethnic Anglicans to explore vocations.** This is a sad reflection on the Church. The clergy's role is crucial to this process, as enabler, encourager, supporter. Appendix D from *How We Stand* provides information on black Anglicans who are already exercising ministries and other responsibilities in dioceses.

4.10   With respect to the task of fostering vocations to ordination among minority ethnic Anglicans, we think that the recommendations which were made by the Vocations Lay and Ordained Workshop at the 1994 Black Anglican Celebration bear repetition, as they are particularly relevant at the local level.

(a)   Ministers should be encouraged to identify and nurture gifts of all people.

(b)   Involve minority ethnic people in visible tasks, including decision-making processes.

(c)   Church should recapture the ministry of discerning vocations.

(d)   Use prayer as a tool in the discernment process.

(e)   Use minority ethnic clergy for short-term placements in white parishes and 'locums'.

(f)   Preach, teach, educate people at parish level. (p. 74 *Roots & Wings*)

The participation of minority ethnic people in the life of the Church

4.11   From autumn 1992-94, the Committee conducted a survey of the 13,000 parishes of the Church in order to ascertain the number of black Anglicans and the extent of their participation in the life of the Church of England. The survey led to the report *How We Stand: A Report on Black Anglican Membership in the Church of England in the 1990s*, and this was made possible due to the major role which the Statistics Department of the Central Board of Finance played in this project.

4.12   The Committee would like to thank those who supported this effort; the diocesan bishops (some of whom wrote articles in their diocesan newsletters recommending the questionnaire to parishes); diocesan secretaries who undertook the circulation of the questionnaires to the parishes; incumbents who took the time to respond (60 per cent of parishes); and the Statistics Department for their role in co-ordinating the project, mailing the questionnaires, analysing the responses and writing the report.

4.13   In the report, black Anglicans are defined as those of Caribbean, African and Asian backgrounds. The survey indicated that there are 27,000 black Anglicans in the Church of England; adjusting for the missing parishes, there are probably 15,760 adult worshippers on any Sunday and 11,400 children. Whilst the Dioceses of Birmingham, London and Southwark account for the majority of the black Anglican participation within the Church that has been observed in the survey, it must be noted that every diocese has some black Anglican worshippers. The survey also identified the fact that black Anglicans bring a higher proportion of children to church: nationally there are 10 children for every 41 adults in church on a Sunday; among black worshippers, the ratio is 10 children to 16 adults.

4.14   However, many black Anglicans were not registering on the electoral rolls and non-membership of electoral rolls may be one reason why they were numerically under-represented on PCCs and synods. In parishes where there are black Anglicans, they make up 4.5 per cent of usual attendance, on average, but only 3 per cent of the electoral roll. In the same parishes, 4.4 per cent of the churchwardens are black and 3.4 per cent are PCC members. Churchwardens are elected by everyone in the parish, while PCC members and deanery synod representatives are elected only by those on the electoral roll. The question remains as to why not all black Anglicans are on electoral rolls.

4.15   Given the role of incumbents in the parish, CMEAC was very disappointed at the response of some to the survey questionnaire. *There were incumbents who wrote quite disparagingly; some portrayed the survey as divisive: 'I try to be friendly and to help all of them, and the colour of their skin is as irrelevant as the coats they are wearing'; 'We are colour blind in this parish and therefore treat this form with the contempt it deserves'; Another comment: 'When does black cease to be black and become coffee, brown, chocolate etc. etc.'; and yet another: 'Until this questionnaire I had not even considered racial identity as important. It isn't – so why this?' Another vicar considered the survey as mischief-making and replied accordingly: 'There are approximately 2,500 souls in this benefice, I will not co-operate with this kind of mischief-making statistical analysis.' With respect to black leadership, one vicar commented: 'Any Seeds of Hope for this parish will fall on stony ground until some black leadership emerges.'* The question might well be asked to what extent were vicars really helping that leadership to emerge? It is quite clear that there is still a great deal of educational work to be done.

4.16   On the whole there were positive responses to the survey, and many not only completed the questionnaire but also supplied additional information. Some vicars were glad that the Committee had raised the issues and were looking forward to the results/recommendations, several were concerned about the need for black participation and leadership at the parish level, and one vicar asked about leadership at the national level of the Church. The absence of black clergy was commented on and the need for vocations to ordained ministry. With respect to good practice, one vicar spoke of the increase in the number of black adult-children attending church and the likelihood of a black person being elected on to the PCC; another reported that their parish audit was taking place and multi-racial issues were firmly on the agenda. One parish was hoping to employ a full-time Christian Asian worker and was asking for the Committee's fullest support and prayers. One vicar wished us well in our quest for the truth. The genuine concerns of many vicars might best be reflected in a comment by one: *The Asian and Afro-Caribbean worshippers at St John's are part of the worship and work of the Church. In town they are being harnessed as links between the Church and their ethnic groups in the parish'; 'Our Church of England capacity to affirm black people may reflect our success/failure as a Church.'*

4.17   The Dioceses of Birmingham, Coventry and Southwark conducted their own research in parishes. Guildford Diocese also conducted a limited survey (two deaneries on black membership). In Bristol, the Keyboard Project used the statistical information on the diocese from *How We Stand* to write a summary report. The Archdeacon's Articles of Enquiry also included a question about black Anglican participation.

4.18   With respect to the General Synod, 13 minority ethnic Anglicans were elected to serve in 1995. They are from the dioceses of Birmingham (3), Lichfield (1), Liverpool (1), Manchester (2), Newcastle (1), Oxford (2), Ripon (1), and Southwark (2). Members are from a wider spread of dioceses and for the first time minority ethnic Anglicans are among Synod members representing Lichfield and Newcastle Dioceses. Nevertheless it should be noted that there has been a decrease in 1995, as compared with the 1990 General Synod Elections when 14 minority ethnic members were successful. It was extremely disappointing that given the ethnic make-up of the Diocese of London no minority ethnic Anglican candidate was successful in the 1995 General Synod Elections.

4.19   The Trumpet Call reminds the Church that minority ethnic people are Christians, minority ethnic people are Anglicans.

> *Our ethnic origins may lie in Africa, the Americas, Asia, or the Caribbean Islands, and a few of us are visitors from these lands, but mostly we ourselves are English, a large proportion of us born in England, and glad to be Anglicans here in partnership with white Christians. We belong to this land and to every corner of it. Make us more visible within the life and leadership of*

our Church. Racism contradicts our Lord's command to love our neighbours as ourselves. It offends the fundamental Christian belief that every person is made in the image of God and is equally precious in His sight. Racism has no place in Christ: it creates nothing but hatred and fear. (Trumpet Call, the final statement of the 1994 Black Anglican Celebration for the Decade of Evangelism)

4.20   Minority ethnic Anglicans have an earnest desire truly to belong to the Church of England; in fact many were born into the faith and know no other. In parishes where their diversity of gifts has been recognised the Church has been enriched. In many parishes that has not happened and people have expressed a great deal of pain. We still hear reports of marginalisation – Chinese, Pakistan, Indian and other Anglicans who are advised to set up their own churches. 'We don't want to be part of a black-led or separate church. If we did we would have joined one long ago. We positively want to be in a black and white church' (Participants at the Bishop of Birmingham's Celebration for Black and Asian Anglicans). This attitude of exclusion is reminiscent of the arrival of African-Caribbean people in Britain in the 1950s and 1960s. Should the Church of England continue to lose more dedicated Anglicans because of exclusion which is again being meted out to others who are also part of the body of Christ?

4.21   *Seeds of Hope* had expressed concerns about the need for liturgical aids: '*The special concerns of Asian Anglicans should be identified and addressed. In one diocese we were told of the need for liturgical aids i.e. liturgies in Asian languages.*' In 1995, Partnership for World Mission (PWM) in collaboration with CMEAC held a one-day consultation which looked at the Church of England and Asian Christians. The concerns which Asian Christians raised were similar in many respects to concerns which CMEAC has been addressing constantly. There were also issues to do with language, music and liturgy, converts to the Christian faith, Asian Christian theology, and the deployment and support of clergy and special workers in areas of Asian communities.

4.22   With respect to minority ethnic Anglican youth, those who were present at the 1994 Celebration spoke of the need for recognition and affirmation, and the importance of attracting and retaining young people. Within the Church, just as in society, minority ethnic youth experience double discrimination. *'I am black. I was born here and I am English but white people do not want to accept us. As a young black male I am looked upon by many as a criminal every time I walk down the street'* (man aged 30, quoted in *The Financial Times*, 15 December 1995). This often results in young people getting fed up and leaving the Church.

4.23   The Church must work at valuing not only majority ethnic but also minority ethnic youth. All our young people need to be supported as they are the Church of today, as well as of the future, and their contribution is vital to its growth. The question could well be asked how is the Church reaching out to young people, especially minority ethnic youth, in the Decade of Evangelism? *Roots & Wings* provides practical ways of addressing these matters in the workshop report on minority ethnic participation in the Church of England; also other workshop reports on confidence building; and strategies towards encouraging the Church to be more inclusive.

4.24   The General Synod Board of Education's report *Youth A Part: Young People and the Church* identifies in detail many of the concerns of young people and suggests very positive ways of how the Church can be more inclusive of all its young people.

CMEAC's Diocesan networks

4.25   During the last six years, with the assistance of diocesan bishops, the Committee has developed a network of **diocesan Link People** in 42 of the 44 dioceses. These persons are minority ethnic Anglicans who are nominated mainly by bishops to serve in a voluntary capacity, as a link between the diocese and the Committee's work.

4.26   The network has gained in confidence, and members give a great deal of their time as they are very committed to the Church and its ministry. Some members have become more involved and are now members of General Synod, diocesan and deanery synods, as well as other decision-making bodies. They also encourage other minority ethnic Anglicans to become involved.

4.27   In many dioceses the Link People have been at the forefront of pressing for change within the structures for a more inclusive Church, as well as affirming and supporting minority ethnic Anglicans. In the latter respect, conferences have been held in the Dioceses of Birmingham, Blackburn, Bristol (Swindon area), Coventry, Lichfield, Lincoln, Liverpool, London, Sheffield, Winchester and Peterborough.

4.28   The **Young Minority Ethnic Anglican Group** is also an important aspect of the Committee's link with dioceses. These are minority ethnic Anglicans between the ages of 18 and 35 years who have been nominated by diocesan bishops to represent their dioceses. Currently 20 dioceses are represented, and the Group is growing. The General Synod Board of Education has provided financial, as well as staff support through its Youth Officers, to CMEAC in the development of its young group. The Committee has been encouraged by the fact that the 1996 National Youth Sunday Resources Pack used as its theme Racial Justice. The Church of England Youth Services assisted with this ecumenical pack, and they also involved two members of CMEAC's Youth Issues Group in its preparation: Ms Josile Munro and Captain Rayman Khan.

4.29   The Diocese of Southwark has been outstanding in the annual Youth Conferences which the Southwark Race Relations Commission has been hosting over the last ten years. In 1996 over 70 young adults attended the conference which was held in Derby, and included young people from London as well as St Albans Dioceses.

4.30   CMEAC's networks are a considerable asset and resource to the development of the work. Several members have attended courses organised by the General Synod Communications Unit. Members bring considerable experience, skills and knowledge from a range of vocations and professions.

4.31   *Roots & Wings*, the report of the 1994 Black Anglican Celebration for the Decade of Evangelism, provides a number of recommendations from workshops on strategies for encouraging minority ethnic Anglican participation. In London Diocese, the Black Anglican Concerns Committee is creating and setting up a parish-based course entitled 'Enjoying Our Blessings'. This course aims to enable (black/white) Church groups to work towards a greater understanding in a nonthreatening context. The course has had a successful 'trial run' in Enfield Deanery. Blackburn Diocese is producing and promoting a study pack on race relations. CMEAC's study pack entitled *Seeds of Hope in the Parish* should also help parishes to engage with the issues and explore ways and means of encouraging increase in participation by minority ethnic Anglicans. This pack was compiled with the help of one of the General Synod Board of Education's Adult Education Advisers.

Relationships with other Minority Ethnic Christians

4.32   We understand that in some dioceses, Race and Community Relations Committees include members from other mainstream denominations, as well as black majority churches. Issues of racial justice have an impact on all minority ethnic people regardless of their denomination, so that any efforts at collaboration are to be welcomed, and should be emulated wherever possible at the parish level.

4.33   In tackling these matters, it must be borne in mind that although this spirit of ecumenism is commendable, the Church of England has a responsibility to ensure that the agenda of combating racism within its own structures at all levels does not get lost in the wider agenda.

4.34   With respect to sharing and sale of church buildings, in some parishes there are some models of good practice. For instance, from time to time guest and host churches share worship and there is generally a good relationship. Nevertheless there are many instances of poor relationships between host churches and guest churches and it has been reported that in some instances extortionate rents are charged by the host church. This is a great concern to guest churches many of whom desperately require the use of a building for worship.

4.35   Arising out of these concerns, in 1993, on behalf of the General Synod, the Secretary General together with the General Secretary for the Churches Together in England (CTE) organised a one-day consultation. The Working Party which was set up subsequently made a number of recommendations, including the publication of a leaflet, as well as a more detailed document with guidelines on the sharing of a building (church or hall) and the buying of a redundant building, for both host and guest churches. These are available on request from CTE and can help parishes planning to go into partnership with black majority Churches.

Relationships with People of other Faiths

4.36   There are models of good practice in many dioceses, and in some dioceses there is more concentration on inter-faith relations than on race and racial justice issues. Inter-faith advisers have been appointed in some dioceses supported by Inter-Faith Committees. These committees often deal not only with religious matters and how to relate a spirit of understanding, but also tackle racial justice issues such as immigration and policing within the community.

4.37   The Inter-Faith Consultative Group of the General Synod Board of Mission has published a booklet entitled *Communities and Buildings: Church of England Premises and Other Faiths*. This follows up other reports, namely *Towards a Theology for Inter-Faith Dialogue; 'Multi Faith Worship'? Communities and Buildings: Church of England Premises and Other Faiths*

> sets out the course of discussion on the subject within the
> British Churches for the last 25 years (Chapter 2); asking how
> the Scriptures may speak to us about it (Chapter 3); and out-
> lining how Christians have thought through history about holy
> place and property (Chapter 4). We have reviewed how people
> of other faiths themselves understand sacred space, and what
> they are looking for in acquiring a building (Chapter 5), and
> noted the experience of English churches in sharing buildings
> with other Christian Church bodies and the relevant practice of
> other Christian denominations (Chapter 6). We have made our
> recommendations about disposal (Chapter 7) and about use
> (Chapter 8), and finally offered a short bibliography.

4.38   In some parishes there is good practice, as the parish had estab-
lished contacts with people of other faiths; in others, there had been no effort at making contacts. We were able to discern this from the response to the Survey of Black Anglicans as the questionnaire which was circu-

lated to all incumbents did include a question asking 'How many other places of worship are there in your parish? Roman Catholic, Methodist, Baptist, URC, House churches, Black Independent, Jewish, Muslim, Hindu, Other.'

4.39   The Church of England has worked, and continues to work, at building good inter-faith relations at the national, as well as some diocesan and parochial levels. Parishes wishing to work with other faiths can draw on relevant models of good practice rather than reinvent the wheel. Bishop John Taylor's note of caution given in the first Lambeth Inter-Faith Lecture in 1977 bears repetition as he urged patience and persistence in our attempts to understand one another:

> *This is a more exacting exercise than any of us would wish for, because every human being finds it difficult to sustain contradictions and live with them. Instinctively we either try to destroy what is opposed to our understanding of truth, or we pretend that the antithesis is unreal. ... It takes a high degree of maturity to let the opposites co-exist without pretending that they can be made compatible.*

The Church and Racial Justice Issues

4.40   In addressing the launch of the Racial Justice Forum of the Churches' Commission for Racial Justice (CCRJ), Mr Philip Mawer, Secretary General of the General Synod, spoke of the commitment which Churches must display in supporting racial justice. He said:

> *Nor can the Christian Churches hope themselves to remedy racial injustice. But they have to engage wholeheartedly and unambiguously in pressing for racial justice. True justice and the equality of all in the sight of God lie at the heart of the Christian Gospel. We cannot be Christian and accept racial intolerance.*

4.41   The Church of England has a widespread network which could be very useful in addressing issues of social, as well as racial justice. Through the General Synod Board for Social Responsibility, the Church of England has led delegations about immigration matters to the Government. Bishops have spoken out in the House of Lords on several occasions, as in the case of the recent Asylum and Immigration Bill. Some dioceses, e.g. Gloucester, offered financial assistance to those who could not afford the registration fee in order to acquire permanent status in response to the 1987 deadline. From time to time parishes have offered sanctuary to people under the threat of deportation.

4.42   There is evidence that racial justice issues are being tackled in some dioceses and parishes. Ecumenical conferences in racial justice issues have been held in dioceses such as Exeter and Lincoln. We were pleased to hear that the Dioceses of Liverpool and Leicester continue to give annual grants to the CCRJ's Projects Fund.

4.43   We are hoping that many more parishes will commemorate Racial Justice Sunday which is held annually in September, as well as support the Projects Fund. The study pack which is published annually by CCRJ provides reflections on the Lectionary readings, prayers and activities which can be undertaken by the parish in witnessing for racial justice. The Churches' Commission for Racial Justice reminds us that Racial Justice Sunday offers an opportunity for all Christian communities and Churches in Britain and Ireland to join together in **reflection** on racial justice issues, in **prayer** to enable a Christian response, in **fundraising** for the continued support of national and local initiatives, and in a commitment to action. It is good that the Board for Social Responsibility's Race and Community Relations Committee has made the work of publicising Racial Justice Sunday an important part of its agenda; through their efforts, every parish should have received information about Racial Justice Sunday.

4.44   Racial Justice Forums have been set up in Lincolnshire, Southwark and also by the Churches' Commission for Racial Justice.

4.45   In May 1994, the Archbishop of Canterbury was able to get the endorsement of Church leaders in Britain, as well as Church leaders from fifteen other countries for a European Church Leaders' Statement. In it, he said:

We reject any suggestion of superiority or movement towards exclusiveness which would deprive others of a place in the new Europe, whether they have been here for sometime, have a human right to enter or have sought safety from persecution or conflict. ... Racism – the assumption of superiority and the exercise of dominant power against those of different ethnic background – is a sin. We call on all Christians, and we invite those of other faith communities, to work to eradicate racism from ourselves, our churches, our countries and our continent. This process should be carried out in the spheres of housing, health, employment, immigration and refugee policy, and all other relevant areas.

4.46   We wish to emphasise the fact that racial justice issues are relevant to all communities and not only in areas where there is a concentration of minority ethnic people. 'The connection between worship on a Sunday and how people work through their faith in the week must be made, as policy makers (many of whom live in mainly rural areas) make decisions which affect minority ethnic communities' (*Seeds of Hope*, 5.48).

CHAPTER V

1994 Black Anglican Celebration for the Decade of Evangelism: a view from the centre

5.1   The first Committee for Black Anglican Concerns was set up in 1987, in response to *Faith in the City*. During its term of office, the Committee had discussed the possibility of hosting a conference for black Anglicans, and had started to plan such an event.

5.2   However, given the fact that by 1990 the Committee would be reconstituted, it was agreed that this task should be handed over to the new Committee.

5.3   The idea of a conference was approved by the Committee appointed in 1991. The conference was scheduled for 1994; planning began in earnest for a full weekend event to which parishioners, as well as diocesan bishops and other key people in the diocese, would be invited. The decision was taken that the event should be called a 'Celebration' as the main objective would be to recognise, celebrate and rejoice in the diversity of gifts which black Anglicans bring to the Church, and also to plan strategies towards using black Anglicans in the Decade of Evangelism. The Celebration was mainly for black Anglicans from dioceses, e.g. Link Persons, the Young Black Anglican Group, representatives from parishes and individuals. Delegates would represent the 44 dioceses of the Church of England and leaders of the Church would be involved as listeners, as participants in dialogue, and also in effective solidarity, decision-making and action. Observers from Church of England organisations were invited, as well as observers from other Churches. There were nearly 400 people present at the Celebration, which was held at the University of York on the weekend of 20-24 July. Over 30 bishops participated, including the Archbishops of Canterbury and York. A full report has been published on the Celebration entitled

Roots & Wings. Appendix E of this report sets out the final statement, the Trumpet Call, addressed to the Church of England and its leaders, to our English society, to ourselves, and to our God.

5.4   Only a few of the comments can be recorded here from the scores of letters and telephone calls which the Committee received after the Celebration. These were as follows:

> *'With this Celebration the Church of England took a great step, without precedent in its history.'*
>
> *'Black and white people celebrating together in the awareness that our liberation is bound up with each other.'*
>
> *'I stepped into the unknown, but had a wonderful thought provoking weekend, and was very glad that I had the opportunity to be there.'*
>
> *'We participated fully with enthusiasm both young and old, I was impressed by the number of young people who were present.'*
>
> *'Together we criticised the Church, our Church, this Church: for its lack of open support for its minority ethnic members. For forsaking what we consider are its responsibilities to fully accommodate us within its embrace. For underestimating the power of racism practised against black Anglicans of all shades, both within and outside its direct control, in both its open and oblique forms; for its failure to speak against policies which, in negative ways, disproportionately affect our needs in such areas as health, education, housing, criminal justice and immigration; for its continued failure to embrace our spirituality; for its failure to provide us with sustaining comfort and support when we suffer at the hands of bigots who condemn and discriminate against us, simply because of the colour of our skins.'*
>
> *'Throughout the weekend there was a feeling of belonging and togetherness.'*
>
> *'It was an occasion of joy, encouragement and hope.'*

'The greatest significance of the Celebration was the fact that it happened and was so joyfully vital and vibrant. The atmosphere of acceptance determined a strong recognition and affirmation of the diverse richness that is to be found in the Church of England, particularly in terms of ethnic and cultural variations.'

'One could have wished that the Church of England had been aware and sensitive enough to hold some such gathering as this 20 years ago.'

'If we really do believe in an inclusive Church we are going to have to work very hard to achieve it.'

What has happened since? How have the dioceses and parishes responded?

5.5   The Celebration was undoubtedly a success and left an indelible impression on participants. This has led to a number of positive initiatives. In several dioceses, bishops held debriefing meetings; some held follow-up celebrations/conferences; some dioceses have been re-energised, other dioceses have decided to consider a response to *Seeds of Hope*.

5.6   For minority ethnic Anglicans, it was a time of affirmation, a time of gathering new strength, confidence and new hope. Some have since committed themselves to exploring a vocation within the Church and have been accepted for ordination; some have also gone on to be trained as Readers; others have become much more involved in their local church, some have been elected to serve on diocesan Boards/Councils. We were informed that as a direct result of the Celebration, two members of the Bradford delegation decided to stand for diocesan synod elections. They were successful. Support was given to them both by the diocese in the form of explaining rules and regulations, ensuring the nominations were made correctly etc., and in terms of personal encouragement. One of the two also successfully stood for election from her deanery to the diocesan Advisory Council for Church in Society.

5.7 The response from the CMEAC networks has been very encouraging. During 1996, regional conferences were held in the Dioceses of Coventry and Manchester. The Coventry event was held specially for minority ethnic youth; its theme was 'Youth with a Vision'. Representatives from the Dioceses of Birmingham, Leicester, Lichfield, Oxford and Peterborough were also involved. The theme of the Manchester Conference was 'Challenge, Request and Demand – a day of learning and sharing experience and expertise'. This was a follow-up to the Liverpool Conference held in 1995, and included participants from Chester, London, Liverpool, Manchester, Sheffield, Southwell and Wakefield.

How has CMEAC responded to the Celebration?

5.8 The Celebration led to the redesignation of the Committee from the Committee on Black Anglican Concerns to the **Committee for Minority Ethnic Anglican Concerns**, which is a more inclusive term. **It has also led to a review of the Committee's Terms of Reference which now include the whole question of vocations, theology, liturgy and worship.** The Celebration was meant to be a rallying of the dioceses; it has also resulted in a rallying of the Committee with respect to its response to the needs of minority ethnic Anglicans.

5.9 The Committee has set up a Minority Ethnic Anglican Liturgy Group which is exploring the following:

- ways and means of galvanising and bringing together our rich diversity of gifts – music, poetry, art, drama, dance – the arts as an offering to the Church;

- how to release people to glorify God within the structures;

- how to make a contribution to the discussion on liturgies in the Church of England, as all liturgies are going to be revised in the year 2000.

5.10 In this connection, the Liturgy Group held a one-day consultation earlier this year to which interested persons including liturgists were invited. The theme of the consultation was 'Liturgical Expression as a Gift to the Church'.

5.11   This project has come about as a result of the opinions expressed by many participants at the Celebration, as well as the keen interest displayed by the Archbishop of Canterbury, who stated in his keynote speech:

> *I have long had a great desire to see these diverse forms of spirituality, central in music, expressed more widely within our Church. I believe it is a dimension that will not only enrich our worship and liturgical life but will also add something exciting to our evangelism.*

The Archbishop of Canterbury has promised his support for work which is developed in this area.

CHAPTER VI

Recommendations and conclusions

6.1   We wish to acknowledge that the Church of England has made progress in the task of combating racism in its structures, five years on since the publication and debate of Seeds of Hope. The good practice which is presented throughout *The Passing Winter* is indicative of what has been achieved.

6.2   In Chapter I we gave several reasons why it was important to write a sequel to *Seeds of Hope*. We recognise that dioceses are at different stages of development in this work. This report is meant to be used as a resource by all dioceses, especially those who are finding the task of addressing these issues hard going; also to encourage them to learn from dioceses of a similar profile which are tackling the issues.

6.3   Based on the diocesan progress reports which the Committee received, there are eight dioceses which have either not responded or given a scant response to *Seeds of Hope*. A typical reply was *'nothing involving overt racism has occurred within this diocese'*.

6.4   We wish to acknowledge that several parishes have made efforts to tackle the issues. However, whatever the reasons, many more have not done so. This situation applies also to deaneries. One bishop remarked:

> *In the Church of England we still have to overcome the attitude of inertia and complacency when racial justice issues are raised particularly in rural dioceses; these matters are often perceived as being relevant only in areas where there are black people.*

Some urban dioceses fall short of the expectations of minority ethnic Anglicans within those dioceses. CMEAC still needs to be convinced that work is beginning to happen at deanery and parish levels in all dioceses.

6.5   *The Passing Winter* is therefore meant to identify further what the Church should be doing at all levels in order to give a positive and stronger response to the task of combating racism. The recommendations will be given under three main headings as follows: To the dioceses and their structures; To the parishes; To the General Synod Boards and Councils.

To the dioceses and their structures

6.6   It was clear that positive efforts had been made by some dioceses to discuss, debate and develop effective strategies towards combating racism, in response to the General Synod motion which had commended the recommendations in Chapter V, *Seeds of Hope,* to dioceses, deaneries and parishes. No two dioceses have approached this work in a similar fashion; their response has been dependent on many factors, namely: the perception and commitment or lack of commitment of decision-makers in the dioceses; the level of awareness of decision-makers; the ethnic make-up of the dioceses and the availability of resources.

Recommendation I

6.7   We would recommend that it should be the task of every diocese to engage with these issues, whether or not there are any minority ethnic people living in the diocese. As *Seeds of Hope* reminds us:

> *Today the eradication of racism is a serious task for all of us. It is not some optional liberal gesture towards black people, because racism cannot co-exist with the Holy Spirit either in the human heart or in the Body of Christ.* (The Rt Revd Dr Wilfred Wood, Bishop of Croydon, in the Foreword, *Seeds of Hope*) (See paragraphs 1.1-1.4.)

Recommendation II

6.8   We wish to recommend that dioceses should strive to set up strategies which would integrate this work throughout diocesan

Boards/Councils/Committees. These matters should not be the sole responsibility of the CMEAC diocesan Link Person, or the Committee/Group responsible for these issues. (See paragraphs 2.10-2.12.)

Recommendation III

6.9   We would urge all bishops to commit themselves to this work as the level of importance which Boards/Councils/Committees/diocesan staff/deaneries and parishes attach to these issues will depend to a large extent on the lead which is given at the diocesan level. (see paragraphs 3.8-3.9.) We have been very encouraged by the response of several bishops.

Recommendation IV

6.10   We would recommend that in dioceses where race relations officers have been appointed, whether in a part-time or full-time capacity, the diocese should ensure that the officer concerned has direct access to the bishop and his staff. In addition, proper status should be given to the officer and he or she should not be deemed to be of lesser importance than other heads of departments. Also every effort should be made to provide adequate resources, especially secretarial support. (See paragraphs 3.3-3.5.)

Recommendation V

6.11   We would recommend that dioceses which have not debated *Seeds of Hope* as yet should do so at all levels of the diocese within the next year. (See paragraph 3.16.)

THE CHURCH AS EMPLOYER – ITS COMMITMENT TO EQUAL OPPORTUNITY

6.12   Currently 17 dioceses have equal opportunity policies; some are more comprehensive than others and these have been identified under paragraph 3.38.

Recommendation VI

6.13   We would recommend that dioceses with policies should work at implementing their policies, ensure the training of staff who are meant to implement the policy, as well as provide others with an understanding of the policy. They should also carry out monitoring, as well as evaluation of the policy. Dioceses which have had a policy for some years should seek to evaluate its effectiveness within the next twelve months. (See paragraph 3.39.)

Recommendation VII

6.14   We would recommend that dioceses with inadequate policies, as well as policies which only make reference to race and gender should seek to formulate a comprehensive policy. (See paragraph 3.37.)

Recommendation VIII

6.15   We would also recommend that dioceses without EOPs should undertake to formulate policies. There are several good policies which are available and there is really no need to reinvent the wheel. (See paragraph 3.42.)

Recommendation IX

6.16   We recommend that the diocese puts in place as part of its structures the **monitoring, assessment and evaluation** of the policy on a regular basis. (see paragraph 3.39.)

TRAINING

Recommendation X

6.17   We would recommend that all dioceses need to do a great deal more with respect to training. Dioceses need to commit themselves to raising awareness of race and racial justice issues at all levels among both clergy and laity, through post-ordination, in-service and lay training. Parishes also need to be encouraged about their role in training.

Note in Appendix A the reference to the Bishop of Coventry's letter. (See also paragraphs 3.6-3.11.)

THE DIOCESAN BOARD OF EDUCATION

6.18   We are aware that the diocesan Board's role is an advisory one. However, the education of children and youth on these issues is of immense importance and should not be neglected, or considered a low priority or non-priority.

The Board of Education has been very supportive of the Committee's youth work through funding and support from its youth officers.

Recommendation XI

6.19   We recommend that the Board of Education should continue to identify good practice and communicate these principles to Church schools. We hope that rural schools will take advantage of the resources on 'Valuing Cultural Diversity' which will be produced by CMEAC in collaboration with the General Synod Board of Education. (See paragraphs 3.18-3.27, 4.36-4.39.)

Recommendation XII

6.20   We would urge that all diocesan youth officers, as well as children's officers seek to work with minority ethnic, as well as majority ethnic youth as part of their affirmation of all young people. (See paragraphs 4.22-4.24; 4.29.)

Recommendation XIII

6.21   The General Synod Board of Education should find out the extent to which Institutes or Colleges of Higher Education are addressing the issues raised in paragraph 3.25. Where it is identified that help is needed the appropriate advice and assistance should be offered.

DIOCESAN COMMUNICATION DEPARTMENTS

Recommendation XIV

6.22   We would recommend that every effort should be made by the Church to present positive images of minority ethnic people, instead of the usual stereotypical images.

Recommendation XV

6.23   We recommend that Communications Departments should strive to reflect the ethnic diversity of the Church of England in materials which are published, where this is appropriate. (See paragraph 3.32.)

DIOCESAN RESOURCE CENTRE

Recommendation XVI

6.24   We recommend that these centres which exist in most dioceses should play an important educational role. The diocese should ensure that these centres are well equipped with appropriate materials. (See paragraph 3.30.)

To the parishes

TRAINING

6.25   Training is of such importance that it has been dealt with in Chapters III and IV. It bears repetition here because of the immense influence which clergy have at the parochial level.

Recommendation XVII

6.26   We would recommend that training in racism awareness should be offered to all clergy through post-ordination, as well as in-service training. (See paragraph 4.7.)

Recommendation XVIII

6.27   We would recommend that with respect to minority ethnic clergy and Readers, better efforts should be made to offer pastoral support and training in identified areas of need. (See paragraph 4.8.)

VOCATIONS

6.28   Because of their own understanding of these issues some clergy are on the look out to 'spot talent' and offer support and encouragement to those who would like to explore vocation. However, we have been told that there are examples of parish clergy who are quite indifferent and who really have no wish to encourage, advise or support minority ethnic Anglicans who might wish to put themselves forward for training whether in ordained ministry, lay ministry or religious orders. The encouragement of strong lay leaders among minority ethnic Anglicans will result in more British-born minority ethnic clergy.

Recommendation XIX

6.29   We recommend that the resources of the Simon of Cyrene Theological Institute be utilised in lay leadership training, Access courses and research programmes. (See paragraph 3.11.)

Recommendation XX

6.30   We would urge all clergy to be just as supportive of minority ethnic, as well as majority ethnic parishioners. (see paragraph 4.9.)

> *Let our gifts and calling be recognised and affirmed, our partnership in the life of the Church of England be evident and welcome. We seek to walk confidently in Christ, in line with all of every ethnic group, tribal tongue, who name his name. Let the whole Church of England by deliberate will live the doctrine in practical love. Without it there is no gospel message of God's love for us to live and proclaim.* (Trumpet Call)

Recommendation XXI

6.31   We recommend that determined efforts should be made to encourage and support minority ethnic Anglicans at all levels of the Church. There are resources available (see Bibliography and Resources at the end of this report) which can assist parishes in addressing these issues, so that people can be enabled to participate fully, express their spirituality and use their many gifts within the Church. (see paragraphs 4.13-4.14; 4.19-4.24.) We would urge parishes to utilise the *Seeds of Hope in the Parish* resource pack which has been published by CMEAC.

Recommendation XXII

6.32   We recommend that CMEAC in collaboration with PWM seeks to address the concerns of Asian Anglicans. (See paragraphs 4.20-4.22.)

RELATIONSHIPS WITH OTHER MINORITY ETHNIC CHRISTIANS

Recommendation XXIII

6.33   We recommend that in the spirit of ecumenism, parishes continue to build on relationships which already exist. Parishes which are discussing the possibility of establishing a relationship can draw on the good practice which exists in many parishes. In some instances Churches work together on social issues, sometimes worship together, yet they keep their separate traditions. Both the guest church and the host church sometimes increase in numbers, so that often this relationship has benefited both congregations and their church life. (See paragraphs 4.32-4.35.)

RELATIONSHIPS WITH PEOPLE OF OTHER FAITHS

Recommendation XXIV

6.34   We recommend that parishes located in multi-faith areas consider ways and means of promoting mutual understanding of those from different cultures and faith communities. There is good practice in many parishes and dioceses. Diocesan inter-faith advisers can be consulted on these matters. Where there is no adviser in the diocese, the General Synod Board of Mission's Inter-Faith Relations Secretary can be contacted for information and advice. (See paragraphs 4.36-4.39.)

6.35   There is no room for complacency with respect to racial justice as both in Britain and in the wider Europe racial discrimination, racial harassment and racial violence is on the increase. The Church of England must continue to play a very important role in racial justice work.

Recommendation XXV

6.36   We recommend that parishes should embark on a programme of education about racial justice issues and identify ways of standing alongside people and assisting where there is racial injustice, whether in housing, education, health, employment or immigration matters. The study pack entitled *Seeds of Hope in the Parish* could be helpful in addressing these matters; as well as the 1994 Pre-Celebration study pack published for the 1994 Black Anglican Celebration for the Decade of Evangelism. (See paragraphs 4.40-4.46.)

Recommendation XXVI

6.37   We recommend that parishes commemorate the annual Racial Justice Sunday. Information can be obtained from the Secretary of the RCRC of the Board for Social Responsibility. (see paragraph 4.43.)

To the General Synod Boards and Councils

6.38   With respect to the work of General Synod Boards and Councils, CMEAC's monitoring role has meant that there has been collaboration. On the whole Boards and Councils have been supportive and have endeavoured to address relevant issues. *The Passing Winter* has identified some of the ways in which some Boards and Councils have responded to *Seeds of Hope*.

6.39   We would recommend that within the work of Boards/ Councils/Committees, equal opportunity and an awareness of racial justice issues should form an important criteria for policy formulation and implementation. We would refer especially to the composition of Boards/Councils and their Committees and Working Parties, as well as publications and other materials which are produced by them. Efforts should be made to ensure that they reflect the ethnic make-up of the Church of England. (See paragraphs 3.32; 3.35.)

Conclusions

6.40   In conclusion, *The Passing Winter* has set out to identify how the Church of England has responded to *Seeds of Hope*; to affirm, encourage and heighten awareness; and to identify further what needs to be done in order to combat racism in the dioceses, deaneries and parishes of the Church of England.

6.41   The good practice which is represented throughout the report indicates that in several dioceses the message has been heard and there has been very positive and creative work as various models have been set up with respect to staffing, structures and objectives.

6.42   The report has also shown that there is a hard core of resistance which still responds *'we have no black people; here there is no problem'*. A reply such as this indicates that the Church of England still has considerable ground to cover in addressing these issues through all its structures if this work is to be truly within the lifeblood of the Church's ministry and mission.

6.43   To some extent, the Church has moved on in its thinking at national as well as diocesan levels. Nevertheless, there is still a great deal to be done by way of education and awareness-raising in deaneries and parishes. *The Seeds of Hope in the Parish* resource pack is meant to assist that process. We hope that many parishes will use the resource pack as a guide in order to address the issues. We hope that dioceses will sustain, encourage and support initiatives at diocesan, deanery and parish levels so that this work will be integrated into the structures at all levels. We also hope that the scenario will not be like the cleaning of Westminster Abbey where once the building is completely cleaned it is time to start again from the top.

6.44   As we proceed towards the next millennium, the Committee for Minority Ethnic Anglican Concerns urges the Church of England to set an example by dedicating itself seriously and wholeheartedly to the task of combating racism in its structures, as we live in a society where racism, racial attacks and racial violence are still evil forces in our midst. The Trumpet Call reminds us:

> *Every Christian person in every generation has an individual responsibility to oppose and resist racism in all its forms, striving to reflect that divine love which alone fills our lives with meaning and hope.*

Appendix A

Resolutions from diocesan synods

Some examples of resolutions have been provided which might be useful to dioceses which have not debated *Seeds of Hope* as yet.

Birmingham

'This Synod:

i   Warmly welcomes the report *Seeds of Hope* (GS 977) and commends the recommendations in Chapter V for discussion and action as appropriate by the Councils and Committees of the Diocesan Synod, by Deanery Synods, and by Church Councils throughout the diocese;

ii Invites the Bishop's Council through its Committee for Black Affairs in consultation with the Advisory Council for Adult Education and Training as well as the Lay Employee Agency, to develop and offer learning opportunities in racial consciousness and sensitivity within existing budgets;

iii Notes the unanimous resolution of the new Bishop's Council at its first meeting to undertake itself training in racial consciousness and sensitivity at an appropriate point with the assistance of personnel experienced in this field;

iv Requests the Bishop's Council in consultation with the Committee for Black Affairs and the Board of Finance to consider the practicality and cost of training on racial consciousness and sensitivity for members of Diocesan Councils and Committees, Deanery Synods, and Church Councils, as well as Deans, and Diocesan Board of Finance employees, including a review of the D.B.F. Equal Opportunities Policy previously approved at its 15th October 1986 meeting; and

v   Notes with gratitude the evolving black and white partnership
        in the Diocese and especially the efforts of the Committee for
        Black Affairs constituted following the Bishop's Council's 21st
        January 1987 meeting.'

Diocese of Birmingham Synod
Saturday 14th March 1992

Bristol

'That the report *Seeds of Hope* be received:

That this Synod

a   Invites the Bishop's Council, all diocesan Boards and
        Committees, Councils, Deaneries, Parishes and others to whom
        the recommendations in Chapter 5 are directed, to consider the
        report of the Committee on Black Anglican Concerns;

b   Encourages the Diocesan Bishop in conjunction with the
        Bishop's Council to set up a small group, drawing together all
        interested parties, to consider how the recommendations in
        Chapter 5 can best be implemented through the life and struc-
        tures of the Diocese, and to report back to the Bishop's Council
        by March 1994.'

Diocese of Bristol Synod
Saturday 13th March 1993

Coventry

'That this Synod do:

1   declare its own repentance and acknowledgement of racist atti-
        tudes and calls others to repent of such attitudes.

2   believe racism to be a social evil and a threat to the integrity of the Church.

3   welcome the *Seeds of Hope* report as a timely encouragement to the Church in combating racism within its institutions and structures.

4   urge every parish (especially clergy and lay leaders) and deanery synod members to consider some form of racism awareness training for themselves and asks Bishop's Council and its Equal Opportunities Group to advise on suitable forms of training.

5   recognise that the welcoming and nurturing of black Anglicans is a task for the whole diocese, and therefore urges parishes, as well as those at the Centre, to seek opportunities to encourage and increase active participation by black Anglicans, particularly into leadership roles.

6   welcome the appointment of the new Community Relations Adviser and calls on all members of the Diocese to offer him prayerful support for the task.'

Diocese of Coventry
11th November 1995

In February 1996, the Bishop of Coventry sent a letter to all parishes in which he recorded resolutions from the diocesan synod debate and urged them to act. 'In the meantime I ask you all to take to heart the resolutions from Diocesan Synod whether your parish is a mixed racial and cultural part of Coventry or small village which sees itself as having no need to consider such matters.'

Leicester

'This Synod warmly welcomes *Seeds of Hope* (GS 977) and recognises the opportunity that it presents to build upon its resolution of 16th March 1991 by enabling the Church in the Diocese and in its ecumenical relationships to engage positively and actively with issues of race and justice.

Consequently Synod -

i   affirms that all baptised people are involved together in God's building of a new humanity in Jesus Christ and, therefore, that the call to racial justice is a call to all God's people;

ii   instructs the Race and Community Relations Committee, in consultation with the Diocesan Black Anglican Forum, to develop and offer to the Diocese opportunities for learning about racial consciousness and sensitivity within existing budgets, and urges all Diocesan Boards and Committees as well as deanery and parish bodies to participate in them;

iii   recognises the contribution made by Black people, both of Afro-Caribbean and Asian descent, to the life of the Church, so that it hopes to see Black people assume their rightful place in the decision-making structures, senior positions and hierarchy of the Church of England, and requests the Bishop's Council to keep this situation under review;

iv   authorises the Diocesan Board of Finance to continue to expend a sum not exceeding £1,850 by way of an annual grant to the Commission for Racial Justice of the Council of Churches in Britain and Ireland for the three years 1994-1996.'

Diocese of Leicester Synod
19th March 1994

Oxford

'That this Synod welcomes the report *Seeds of Hope* and commends it for discussion and appropriate action to the deaneries and parishes. It recognises the need to raise awareness of racial issues through education and training in both Church and society and to facilitate fuller black participation at all levels in the process of decision making.

Therefore, this Synod requests the Bishop's Council together with the BSR Race Group to give urgent consideration to the means of promoting racial justice in the diocese, and to report back to the Synod in March 1994.'

Ripon

'That this Synod refers the recommendations contained in the report from the Bishop's Working Party on *Seeds of Hope* to deaneries and parishes for their consideration and comment.' Excerpts from the Bishop's Working Party on *Seeds of Hope,* Report to Diocesan Synod 21st November 1992 are included, the full report can be obtained from the diocese.

We live in a society where often even a mention of racial justice results in assumptions of finger-pointing or allegations of racism. A defensive screen is immediately erected. To what extent does the Church accept Racism in society as part of its concern? It is important to accept that in some parishes work is being done. Unfortunately far too few parishes attached any priority to this work. There are areas where there are no minority ethnic persons and so it is not considered necessary to consider such matters. The Church needs to accept that prejudice and the practice of disadvantaging or advantaging someone solely on the grounds of colour, culture or ethnic origin is still present in British society. By accepting this fact, it must equip itself with the necessary machinery that will enable it to identify, prevent and eliminate such practice. As Christians we must accept that Racial Injustice like any other type of injustice is a sin. None of us are free from this sin. Nor is it an easy thing to talk about. Racial Justice must be a constant concern at parish level regardless of whether there are black people in the congregation or not.

A) Structures (p16)

i)   The Bishop's Council should ensure that each of the 7 areas of work (p15) is clearly identified with specific boards or committees. We recommend:

      (A)   Structures: The Bishops, Bishop's Council and Board of Ministry and Training.

      (B)   Education: The Board of Education.

      (C)   Participation: All.

      (D)   Employment: All and Diocesan Office.

      (E)   Other Black Christians: Board of Mission and Unity.

      (F)   Other Faiths: Board of Mission and Unity.

      (G)   Wider Society: Board for Social Responsibility.

There will be the need for an appropriate body to monitor progress, develop effective diocesan strategies, identify good and bad practice and communicate with all levels of the diocese. Such a body will need to receive reports from diocesan boards and committees about their specific responsibilities.

ii)   Every effort should be made to ensure a black presence on decision making bodies and in all parts of the diocese.

iii)   Issues connected with Racism should be on chapter, deanery synod and parish agendas. Questions at the Archdeacon's visitation will be useful in helping this process.

iv)   At all levels of communication materials should show black people as a natural part of the community.

Sheffield

'That the Synod receive the General Synod report *Seeds of Hope* and the Social Responsibility Committee Report "Black People in the Diocese of Sheffield" and ask the Bishop's Council to advise the Synod on ways in which the recommendations of both reports can be furthered in the Diocese.'

APPENDIX B

Lichfield Diocese Questionnaire

Archdeaconry of Stoke-upon-Trent – Visitation 1995

Black Anglican Concerns

1. As Britain is now a multi-cultural community in what way have you engaged in any of the issues deriving from this?

2. How have you enabled your congregation to welcome people from other cultures?

3. Have you any questions or comments you wish to make about Black Anglican Concerns?

4. Would you welcome a follow-up to your PCC, Synod, Chapter, by the Revd Rose Hudson-Wilkin?

Appendix C

Truro Diocese Questionnaire

Questions posed to parishes as a suggested framework for study by the Rt Revd Michael Ball, Bishop of Truro. Response to *Seeds of Hope*

1. Why do you think there are so few non-white people in Cornwall?

2. Are you happy for your children to form liaisons with partners of another race?

3. Would you object to your church being served by a black incumbent?

4. Would a black family feel welcome in your church?

5. How would you feel if you as a white were outnumbered by black in your church?

6. Is it possible to separate racist issues from those of religion and nationalism?

7. What do you consider is the purpose of this report?

8. How have your views been confirmed or been changed as a result of studying this report?

APPENDIX D Table 6.1 from *How We Stand* (1994)

DIOCESE	Clergy	Readers	Church Army	Churchwardens	
Bath & Wells	0	0	0	0	
Birmingham	5	4	1	27	
Blackburn	2	0	0	0	
Bradford	3	0	0	0	
Bristol	0	0	1	3	
Canterbury	0	0	0	0	
Carlisle	0	0	0	0	
Chelmsford	8	3	1	16	
Chester	1	0	0	0	
Chichester	1	0	0	0	
Coventry	2	1	0	4	
Derby	2	1	0	0	
Durham	0	0	0	0	
Ely	3	0	0	0	
Exeter	0	0	1	0	
Gloucester	0	0	1	1	
Guildford	0	0	0	0	
Hereford	0	0	0	0	
Leicester	4	1	0	3	
Lichfield	7	3	2	7	
Lincoln	0	0	0	0	
Liverpool	2	1	0	3	
London	17	6	0	61	
Manchester	7	1	0	7	
Newcastle	0	0	0	0	
Norwich	0	0	0	0	
Oxford	4	3	1	7	
Peterborough	0	0	0	1	
Portsmouth	2	0	0	0	
Ripon	0	1	0	2	
Rochester	3	0	0	4	
St. Albans	2	1	0	3	
St. Edms & Ipswich	0	0	0	0	
Salisbury	1	0	0	0	
Sheffield	0	0	0	2	
Sodor & Man	0	0	0	0	
Southwark	10	12	9	55	
Southwell	1	1	0	4	
Truro	0	0	0	0	
Wakefield	0	0	0	1	
Winchester	1	0	0	2	
Worcester	1	0	0	0	
York	3	0	0	0	
TOTAL	92	39	17	213	

Black Anglican participation in positions of responsibility

PCC members	Deanery Synod members	Diocesan Synod members	Eucharistic assistants	Sidesmen & women	Group leaders
2	1	0	1	4	2
167	25	6	47	172	147
7	1	0	4	13	6
5	1	0	4	14	7
15	2	0	5	21	7
3	0	0	0	3	0
2	0	0	1	2	3
122	9	2	19	136	39
6	2	0	1	10	4
4	1	0	1	8	1
30	3	1	11	31	10
5	2	0	2	7	5
2	0	0	2	4	2
2	1	1	2	4	4
3	0	0	0	5	0
6	0	0	2	6	2
6	3	0	2	14	5
0	0	0	0	0	1
25	6	2	18	15	7
65	4	1	17	79	20
5	1	0	1	4	0
24	6	2	5	42	8
443	63	6	141	571	141
84	15	3	24	88	23
4	0	0	0	9	0
2	0	0	0	2	0
44	6	1	19	67	18
14	1	0	5	17	7
4	1	1	2	5	0
17	6	2	7	45	4
17	5	0	11	21	14
39	7	0	13	69	26
11	2	0	4	5	5
2	2	0	0	4	3
12	1	0	5	16	8
1	0	0	0	0	0
419	53	8	148	519	129
15	5	2	3	14	5
1	0	0	0	0	0
6	0	0	2	15	3
6	1	0	3	13	3
6	0	0	2	12	3
1	1	0	2	6	1
1654	237	38	536	2092	673

Appendix E

Trumpet Call, final statement
of the 1994 Black Anglican Celebration
for the Decade of Evangelism

When nearly 400 people met for the weekend of 22-24 July, 1994, at the University of York, the Church of England took a step without precedent in its history. This was the first ever national Black Anglican Celebration, convened after three years' planning by the General Synod's Committee for Black Anglican Concerns, and attended by representatives of every diocese, with Bishops from most dioceses, and guests from other churches. Its main purpose was to celebrate and affirm the participation of black Anglican Christians in the task of the Decade of Evangelism, and to enable them to make common cause with each other for this purpose. Two-thirds of the participants were themselves black Anglicans, with an even balance between the sexes, a lay presence far greater than the clerical, and a distribution of ages weighted towards the younger end. The Celebration was addressed by both Archbishops, as well as by practised experts from minority ethnic men and women who gave a hard-hitting lead about the tasks facing black Christians today. The Celebration was enlivened by worship in groups, in plenary, and at York Minster, and also by both sport and an internationally flavoured concert.

However, the main work of the Celebration was done in seventeen workshops, addressing ways in which black Christians may take that place in the Church and in the community to which they are called by God. From the results of this work the black Anglicans with the support of all others at the Celebration issue this trumpet call:

To the Church of England and its leaders, we say:

Black people are people. Black Christians are Christians. Black Anglicans are Anglicans. Our ethnic origins may lie in Africa, the Americas, Asia, or the Caribbean Islands, and a few of us are visitors from these lands, but mostly we ourselves are English, a large proportion of us born in England, and glad to be Anglicans here in partnership with white Christians. We belong to this land and to every corner of it. Make us more visible within the life and leadership of our Church. Racism contradicts our Lord's command to love our neighbours as ourselves. It offends the fundamental Christian belief that every person is made in the image of God and is equally precious in His sight. Racism has no place in Christ: it creates nothing but hatred and fear.

Every Christian person in every generation has an individual responsibility to oppose and resist racism in all its forms, striving to reflect that divine Love which alone fills our lives with meaning and hope. So let all discrimination against us, knowing or ignorant, latent or overt, cease. Let us reach our own fullness in Christ as ourselves. Let our gifts and calling be recognised and affirmed, our partnership in the life of the Church of England be evident and welcome. We seek to walk confidently in Christ, one in him with all of every ethnic group, tribe and tongue, who name his name. Let the whole Church of England by deliberate will live this doctrine in practical love. Without it there is no Gospel message of God's love for us to live and proclaim.

To our English society, we say:

Black people are people. Black English are English. But there is as yet no real equality in jobs, housing, health, educational opportunity or the media and their message. True justice is too frequently missing from police methods and administration of the law. Institutional racism is deeply rooted, and we fear for our children if it is not rooted out. We are here; we are English; we are part of the community. Give us justice.

To ourselves, we say:

We have a responsibility to ourselves, our young people and the wider community to take up the challenges that we have met this weekend. The challenges like growing in confidence and leadership potential; and taking risks in order that we might grow; and offering this confidence as a gift to the whole Church. Risks that will allow us to create our own space and not leave others to create it for us. The risks to use our gifts in whatever way possible especially in the task of Evangelism and Mission. We are ready to play our part in reclaiming our rich Biblical inheritance for both Black and White. We are ready to encourage the Church to live the Christian faith authentically and therefore to confront our society in areas of racial injustices. For us evangelism and caring go hand in hand. We are committed to demonstrating and proclaiming the gospel. We are determined to encourage young black Anglicans to remain and become involved in our Church at all levels.

To our God, we say:

We have sounded our trumpet-call to redress wrongs done to us, yet we are humbled before your love and are only seeking your Glory. Let your trumpet-call now guide our feet, your judgement and justice cry out to the skies. We meet in your love to do your will. We place our cause in your hands. Do your will in us that your world may be transformed. Amen.

Bibliography

Communities and Buildings: Church of England Premises and Other Faiths, Board of Mission of the General Synod of the Church of England, 1996.

Enjoying our Blessings, parish-based course, London Diocese.

General Synod November Group of Session 1991: A Report of Proceedings, Vol. 22, No. 3.

How We Stand: A Report on Black Anglican Membership of the Church of England in the 1990s, The General Synod of the Church of England, 1994.

Roots & Wings: A Report of the Black Anglican Celebration for the Decade of Evangelism, The General Synod of the Church of England, 1994.

Seeds of Hope: Report of a Survey on Combating Racism in the Dioceses of the Church of England, The General Synod of the Church of England, 1991.

Resources

Challenge, Change and Opportunity: The Future of Multi-ethnic Britain, a report on the conference held at the University of Reading, autumn 1994, Runnymede Trust, 1994.

Children and Racism, a ChildLine Study, ChildLine, 1996.

Churches Together in England: Report of a Working Party on the Sharing and Sale of Church Buildings, 1993. Churches Together in England (London Office)

Colour & Spice: Guidelines on Combating Racism in Church Schools, Southwark Diocesan Education Services Ltd., 1994. Available from 48 Union Street, London SE1 1TD

Helen Derbyshire, *Not in Norfolk: Tackling the Invisibility of Racism,* Norfolk and Norwich Race Equality Council, 1994.

Equality Assurance in Schools, Quality, Identity, Society: A Handbook for Action Planning and School Effectiveness, Trentham Books for the Runnymede Trust, 1993.

David Haslam, *Race for the Millennium: A Challenge to Church and Society*, Church House Publishing, 1996.

Integration and Assessment: An Interim Evaluation of College and Course Responses to ACCM Paper No. 22, Advisory Board of Ministry, 1992.

Eric Jay, *Keep Them in Birmingham: Challenging Racism in South-West England*, Commission for Racial Equality, 1992.

National Youth Sunday Resource Pack (Theme: Racial Justice), Catholic Youth Services, 1996.

One Race: A Study Pack for Churches on Racial Violence, Churches' Commission for Racial Justice, 1994.

Jenny Osowae, Lee Bridge and Chris Searle, *Outcast England: How Schools Exclude Black Children*, Institute of Race Relations, 1994.

Race Relations and Racial Justice: Issues for Christians in Devon, Social Responsibility Committee, 1994.

Respect For All: Developing Anti-Racist Policies in a Church School, The National Society, 1996.

Seeds of Hope in the Parish: Study Pack, CMEAC, 1996.

David Udo, *King of Love and Justice: Account of the Life and Contribution of Martin Luther King Jnr: The State of Race Relations in Britain*, African Caribbean Education Resource Centre, 1995.

We Belong to One Another, study packs for Racial Justice Sunday, Churches' Commission for Racial Justice, 1995 and 1996.

John Wilkinson, *Windows on Theology: Church in Black and White*, St Andrews Press, 1993.

Rt Revd Dr Wilfred Wood, *'Notes on Racism Awareness Training'*, Annual Report of Committee for Black Anglican Concerns, 1992.

Rt Revd Dr Wilfred Wood, *Keep the Faith, Baby! A Bishop speaks on Evangelism, Race Relations and Community*, Bible Reading Fellowship, 1994.

Youth A Part: Young People and the Church, National Society/Church House Publishing, 1996.